Sales DNA

Crack the Code to Hire and Retain the 17% Who Can and Will Sell

John C. Marshall, Ph.D.

FREILING
AGENCY

Published by Freiling Agency, LLC.

P.O. Box 1264
Warrenton, VA 20188

www.FreilingAgency.com

PB ISBN: 978-1-969826-27-6
HB ISBN: 978-1-969826-28-3
E-book ISBN: 978-1-969826-29-0

Contents

> "
> Research shows that only
> about 17% of the population possess
> an innate Sales DNA.
> "

INTRODUCTION

Discovering Sales DNA

You can't coach or develop what isn't there.

That's the hard truth I learned after four decades of studying human performance, first on the ice, then in boardrooms across North America. And it's the truth that will either save your sales organization millions of dollars or waste millions in resources.

The $0 Wake-Up Call

I started my business career with zero clients, in a cramped one-room office, and an untested idea based on years of research in athletic performance. I had developed what I called the POP (Personal Orientation Profile), a psychometric assessment designed to predict performance. I was confident in the science, passionate about the concept, and relatively naive about the realities of business and sales.

After the first month, my wife asked the question every entrepreneur who has attempted to create a new start up dreads: "How much money did we make?" The answer was a brutal $0. I had a well researched assessment tool, solid research credentials, and absolutely no revenue to show for it. That moment taught me something every business owner learns. You need sales to survive.

The top line that keeps the lights on, pays the bills, and validates whether your idea has any real-world value.

Sitting in that tiny office, staring at my bank statement, I realized I had become a case study in my own research. I had the knowledge and the tools, but I lacked the most critical element for business success: the ability to sell. What I discovered next didn't just save my business, it changed everything I thought I knew about human performance in competitive environments.

The Pattern That Changes Everything

My journey began playing competitive hockey, coaching it, and eventually studying it from a scientific perspective. I spent years coaching junior hockey, university teams, and even Division 1 hockey in Italy. But it was during my work as a sports psychologist with an NHL team that I noticed something that was obvious but potentially challenged many of the concepts about development and performance.

The top performers not only worked harder than everyone else but what set them apart was how effortless it appeared. Natural. Fluid. Like they were born for the challenge of the highest level of competition and the grind of professional athletics. They had an internal drive that didn't require external motivation. They competed because that is who they were at their core, not because someone told them to or because they were chasing an external reward.

Meanwhile, other players, equally talented on paper, with similar training backgrounds and often superior technical skills failed to live up to their potential and eventually dropped out. They put in the same hours, followed the same training regimens, worked with the same coaches, but struggled every step of the way. They needed constant encouragement, external motivation, and detailed direction to perform activities that came naturally to their high-performing teammates. The difference was something that couldn't be taught or coached or created, it was simply in their DNA.

A similar pattern emerged when I transitioned into selling sales assessment and began working with businesses. Some people have it. Some don't. And no amount of training, coaching, or motivational programs can manufacture what Mother Nature didn't provide in the original genetic blueprint.

My first real sales lesson came during my first presentation to a real estate VP. I was deep into my pitch when he stopped me cold: "Shut up," he said. "I already said yes, but you didn't hear me."

Two ears, one mouth. Use them proportionally.

That simple lesson opened the door to closing the best life insurance company in Canada, then ten more. Our competitive advantage was that we could predict who would succeed and who would fail, then prove it with customized models based on actual performance data.

The Science Behind the POP

Based on my graduate studies and research, it became obvious that personality is a multidimensional concept. It consists of a variety of source traits that are a function of an interaction between genetics and environment. In some cases, extreme environmental factors can outweigh genetics, while in others, strong genetic influences can prevail. As a result, to predict behavior it is necessary to understand both the DNA and the situation. For example, a naturally competitive individual may act differently at home with family, than they would in an athletic setting, a competitive work environment or when guided by someone they respect. The question becomes what aspect of their personality will dominate when someone or some situation doesn't direct their behavior? After decades of research and over 30 million assessments, we have been able been able to identify the core source traits that are predictive of sales performance. Key source traits stabilize in the late teens or early twenties and are a complex interaction between genetics and environment, innate tendencies and learned behaviors. Individuals with Sales DNA are naturally competitive, enterprising, goal oriented, high achievers who commit to daily activities to accomplish their goals. These characteristics are obviously essential in competitive sales positions that require daily prospecting to survive and excel. Individuals who are not naturally competitive will require extra investments in training, coaching, supervision and management to direct their behavior as most sales activities are performed away from the direct influence of a coach. Some coaches are willing to invest the extra time and resources but ultimately learn that it is a much better ROI to invest in naturally competitive individuals Over the years we have learned from many sales leaders that top sales performers are a function of genetics and continuous development through education, training, experience, coaching and hard work.

The critical insight that separates top performers from the rest lies in what happens when no one is watching, when sales professionals are out prospecting, making cold calls, facing objections and trying to engage with potentially unreceptive cold prospects. In those moments, it is their natural Sales DNA that drives behavior and determines success. Research shows that only about 17% of the population possess this innate Sales DNA. The remaining 83% lack it, and while they can be taught techniques and supported by training, coaching, supervisors, management, the investment required is enormous. Some companies make that investment, hoping to develop what nature did not provide, only to discover that it is often a losing battle – one that drains resources and delivers, at best, mediocre results.

The Tale of Two Salespeople

The following two individuals from my early consulting work highlight the contrast between those who possess Sales DNA and those who do not.

The Hockey Star Who Couldn't Score in Sales

I worked at summer hockey schools with a friend who had achieved every hockey player's dream: a successful career as an NHL player with the Pittsburgh Penguins. He had made substantial money during his playing days, invested wisely, and had the financial cushion to survive in a commission-based career. When he decided to transition into financial services, everything looked perfect on paper. He joined a major company as a 100% commissioned based sales representative, had access to extensive training programs, and possessed a natural market of players, coaches, parents, and hockey industry contacts who knew him, trusted him, and respected his success.

Our POP assessment revealed that he wasn't naturally competitive but situational competitive. I am certain a lot of our readers have met some extremely competitive athletes who are acquiescent and mild mannered when they are not in the rink, on the court or on the field. His manager questioned our POP results and hired him anyway convinced that someone who had succeeded at the highest level of professional hockey had to possess the competitive DNA necessary for sales success.

The reality became clear at an athletic banquet months later. We were both presenting, surrounded by hundreds of potential clients, exactly the type of people who would be interested in financial planning and investment advice. When participants approached my friend and asked what he was doing now that his playing career was over, he gave vague responses: "Still considering options" or "Exploring different opportunities." He didn't hand out a single business card, didn't mention his new career in financial services, didn't suggest they call him if they ever needed advice about protecting their financial future. This was a room full of warm prospects, people who already knew and respected him, but he was uncomfortable promoting himself and his new career. Initially, I thought it was simply the situation, but he had the same reluctance in all his prospecting calls if he encountered any objections.

He eventually failed in the role. His frustrated manager called to discuss his disappointment at not being able to get him to prospect, even within his own natural market, people who would have welcomed his call and been genuinely interested in what he had to offer.

The Multi-Million Dollar Performer with High Sales DNA

At a conference in Halifax, I met the #1 insurance sales agent in America, making several million in annual commissions. Walking to a dinner cruise, he introduced himself to strangers: "Nice to meet you. I'm the #1 life insurance salesperson in the USA, and I help people protect their families and plan for retirement. If you ever need advice, here's my card."

I asked him, "Do you do that all the time?"

He looked confused. "Do what?"

That's when it hit me. This wasn't a forced behavior. It was natural. He just did it.

He had five licensed assistants handling new calls, only getting involved with complex cases and high-net-worth clients. After several hours discussing our experiences in hiring and retaining top performers, we both realized that he was the classic self-manager. He was aware of his strengths and his limitations. He was constantly seeking or hiring resources to complement his strengths and maximize his time and energy. He was consciously competent, totally internally motivated as he had achieved all the external motivators of fame, fortune and success. In addition, he continued to upgrade his skills and knowledge in an effort to maximize his potential.

In summary, he was self-motivated, self-confident, self-sufficient, passionate about his product, proud of his company and continually growing. The fundamentals of self-management—the #1 competency of top performers.

The 17% That Drive 80% of Revenue

After tracking millions of sales professionals, the numbers are stark and consistent:

- Only 17% possess high Sales DNA
- These 17% generate 80% of the total revenue
- The remaining 83% struggle in sales roles but have DNA suited for other careers

My father once criticized my focus on revenue: "John, you're a psychologist. You should be helping people, not focusing on money."

I told him, "Dad, I'm in the greatest profession in the world. The more people I help, the more money I make."

For individuals blessed with high Sales DNA who are passionate about their products, sales is challenging, satisfying, and profitable. For those with low Sales DNA, it's a grind for them and the companies that employ them.

Sales DNA = Higher Revenue

My business mentor, president of a large financial services company with a 100% commission-based sales force, had a simple philosophy: "I love writing large commission checks, especially ones bigger than my salary."

He understood a fundamental truth: "Hiring top sales professionals is like hiring revenue and HIGHER revenues."

While CFOs focus on cost containment and profitability, sales leaders focus on the top line. Increasing revenue combined with controlling costs is the most profitable path to growth.

What You'll Discover

This book will share our research findings on the Sales DNA of top performers:

- How to assess it accurately
- How to coach and develop it
- The ROI of investing in natural talent
- Why 80% of your revenue comes from 17% of your people

The science is clear. The data is overwhelming. Many of the ideas presented in this book have been developed and learned through consulting and workshops with top sales leaders and sales performers. As a result, it is a very applied book but based on solid psychological principles. At times it will simply be reinforcing the characteristics and experiences of the readers who are successful in sales or a sales environment.

We thank you for the ideas, but we don't share royalties.

Enjoy the book.

" When you're operating within your
Career DNA, something magical happens:
your energy investment becomes
less than your results. "

CHAPTER 1

Sales DNA

The Career DNA Reality

We believe you can achieve anything you set your mind to. The real question isn't whether it's possible, it's what price you're willing to pay to succeed.

Your DNA sets the foundation for your potential to become a top performer in any path you choose. Education, training, coaching, experience, and relentless hard work help bring that potential to life. But potential isn't a simple on-off switch, it's a continuum that defines not only how far you can go, but also how much effort it will cost you to get there.

Career potential is best seen as a spectrum from poor, to average, to excellent. The stronger your natural DNA for a specific career, the faster and closer you move toward realizing that potential. Even more important, your return on investment multiplies. When you operate in your natural DNA zone, every hour of training, every coaching session, and every challenge doesn't just add to your growth, it compounds it exponentially.

But here's the challenge: at some point along the continuum, the price becomes too steep, and people burn out. Burnout happens when the energy you put in no longer matches the results you get out. It becomes a poor return on energy. Once you're in an energy deficit, the deeper it grows, the faster you hit the wall.

The ROE Principle (Return On Energy)

In education, we see this energy deficit play out every semester. Many students are steered into career paths that don't align with their natural strengths, forcing them into courses that drain their energy without delivering equal results. This mismatch explains the alarming dropout rates among first-year college students and the high failure rates in demanding fields. When students fight against their natural DNA, the struggle isn't just academic. It rapidly depletes their mental and emotional reserves in ways that can't be sustained.

Business environments tell the same story. Poor hiring decisions and mismatched career choices result in high turnover rates and heavy use of employee assistance programs. Companies spend millions of dollars dealing with burnout, poor performance, and the cascading effects of failure on employee confidence and stress levels. Everyone loses. The individual struggles with diminished self-worth, and the company wastes money while damaging its employer brand.

When your energy investment equals your results, you are in a fragile state. Minor variations in daily experiences, both personal and professional, can flip your return from positive to negative.

However, when you're operating within your Career DNA, something magical happens: your energy investment becomes less than your results. You are literally getting more out than what you are putting in. You are on a roll, and success becomes self-reinforcing. This is what people mean when they say, 'you'll never work another day in your life.' It's not that the work stops being challenging, it's that the challenge fuels you instead of draining you.

The Two Components of Career DNA

Career DNA has two critical components that predict Performance and Retention:

Component #1: Fit to the Career (Performance)

This is your natural ability to excel at the core activities that drive success in a specific role. In sales, that means an innate drive to prospect, compete, close deals, and persist through objections, even when others might perceive those same situations as rejection.

Component #2: Fit to the Environment (Retention)

This is how well you match to the coach, team, and corporate culture. You can have exceptional Sales DNA, but if you work under a micromanaging boss who stifles your style or in a culture that clashes with your values, your performance and engagement will suffer.

The best examples come from professional sports. We have all seen star players traded to a new team, only to underperform or, conversely, seen underachievers suddenly thrive in a new environment. In some cases, a single star joins a new team and lifts the performance of everyone around them. The same dynamic plays out in sales organizations every single day.

The Admission Ticket Principle

Sports also provides the clearest illustration of DNA's role in career success. If you don't have the minimum level of talent, what we call the "Admission Ticket," no amount of hard work, coaching, training, or knowledge will lead to success. You will exhaust yourself trying to compete against people for whom the activities come naturally.

If you do have the "Admission Ticket" and work hard, you might succeed by outperforming others with similar or higher DNA levels who don't apply themselves. The old saying holds: "hard work outperforms talent when talent stops working hard."

The very best performers in sports, sales, or any performance-driven field bring the complete package. They have the DNA, they put in the work, and they constantly sharpen their skills to realize their full potential. What sets them apart is their ability to draw on hidden reserves when the pressure is highest. Many call it resilience or grit, but in truth, it's simply DNA revealing itself under stress.

The Sales DNA Reality

My personal experience spans sales and competitive athletics. Both are performance-based careers with objective measures where there are no hiding places. Top performers are responsible for their performance and accountable for their results.

This book focuses on Sales DNA because sales offers the greatest career opportunity for those blessed with it and the costliest mistake for both individuals and organizations when it's missing. These insights come from selecting, training, and coaching thousands of sales leaders, working with millions of sales professionals, and consulting with hundreds of top sales organizations across every type of distribution system.

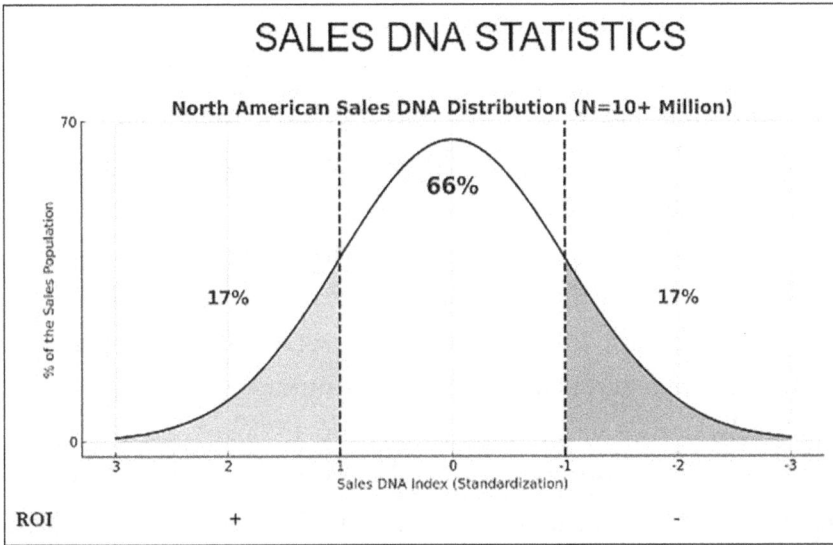

SALES DNA STATISTICS

North American Sales DNA Distribution (N=10+ Million)

66%

17%

17%

% of the Sales Population

Sales DNA Index (Standardization)

70

0

3 2 1 0 -1 -2 -3

ROI + -

As illustrated in the above graph, in any population, 17% fall into the high potential category, 66% cluster in the average range, and 17% occupy the low potential area. Within that 66% average group, roughly 16% trend slightly below average, and 16% slightly above average. With the remaining 34% in the average category.

When it comes to return on investment, the biggest waste of resources in any sales organization stems from attempting to develop individuals who simply don't have the DNA to perform at the highest levels. Lower performers aren't just poor investments, they are actually a cost center that drains resources from your top producers.

The 80-20 Sales Reality

Our benchmark studies consistently demonstrate that 80% of revenue comes from the 17% of salespeople with high Sales DNA, with a minor contribution from the 16% who score slightly above average. When you factor in infrastructure costs, IT, marketing, legal, service, training, HR, management, and leadership, the lower and below-average producers are generating negative returns for the company.

Therefore, the earlier you can identify potential, the sooner your talent acquisition process can focus on 17% rather than wasting time with the 83% who are average, below average, or poor. Effective screening strategies eliminate the bottom 17% while selection processes identify the top 17%.

Here's the irony: advances in AI and technology designed to automate the recruitment process have inadvertently increased the volume of average candidates, overwhelming recruiters and hiring managers. Instead of screening for quality, recruiters are forced to sift through the 83% rather than focusing on the 17%. This leads to hiring average potential candidates who then get handed off to trainers and coaches, forcing these professionals to invest substantial resources for marginal returns. All our major clients know how to develop and train skills and competencies. They also know how to coach potential and maximize performance. So rather than play the blame game where coaches blame trainers and trainers blame recruiters for poor performers, we instead have a high-performance culture.

Sales DNA and Benchmark Studies

The following three benchmark studies demonstrate the relationship between Sales DNA and revenue for a small, a medium and an enterprise level client. A benchmark study analyzes the relationship between Sales DNA and the actual performance of an existing sales team. The objectives of the study are:

1. Identify the Ideal Sales Candidate (ICP) To establish the ICP, we have a group of high and low performers complete the POP™ assessment to investigate the characteristics that differentiate between the 2 performance groups.
2. Customize the prediction model for the client. Based on the factors that differentiate between the 2 groups we develop a customized algorithm that predicts both the low and the high performers.
3. Demonstrate the ROI of replacing the low Potential performers with high performing candidates. We then highlight the revenue lift achieved by replacing low performers with high performers.

Small Business Benchmark

We studied a company with 27 sales agents and created a Sales DNA snapshot using our customized Predictor Score algorithm. We used a simple green, yellow, and red stoplight system for future selection: green represented the 17% with high Sales DNA, yellow the 66% average performers, and red the 17% low potential performers.

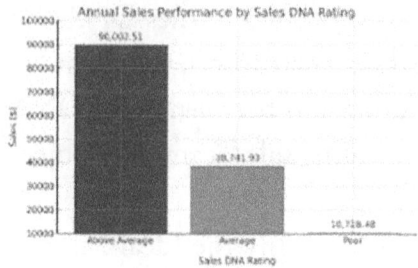

**Small Business Benchmark
(ROI Case Study)**

Selecting Ideal Candidates

Replacing the 9 Agents scoring POOR with
Green Light Agents is projected to increase
the average monthly sales by $59,456.00

ROI: Average Annual Sales
Increase

$715 K

As illustrated in the graph, if the client simply replaced the nine sales agents who scored in the red zone (the poor category on the right side of the graph) with high performers (above average categoryon the left side of the graph), this company could increase monthly sales by $59,456 and annual revenue by $715,000.

Mid-Size Business Benchmark

In this mid-size example, we separated the top performers into green lights and Golden Eagles (left side of the graph). The Golden Eagles had both the DNA and previous experience. This helped our client attract and hire more of the best performers. We will discuss coaching and retaining Golden Eagles in a future chapter.

Mid-Size Business Benchmark ROI Case Study

Selecting Ideal Candidates

Replacing 8 Advisors scoring red on the POPy with Golden Eagle Advisors is projected to increase the average monthly sales to $12,063,530

ROI: Average Annual Sales Increase

$144 M

Again, the ROI by replacing the 8 low performing agents(represented on the right side of the graph) with Golden Eagles would increase the average monthly revenue by $12,063,630 or $144 million annually. This tends to get the attention of the sales leaders and the executive team.

Enterprise Business Benchmark

We conducted a study with a large International bank that measured performance by Net New Business: New sales minus client losses and terminations. The data revealed two eye-opening findings: lower-performing representatives were making new sales but losing more clients than they were gaining (a negative net gain).

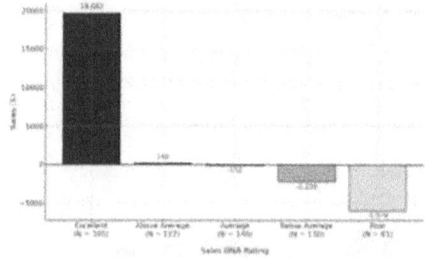

ENTERPRISE BUSINESS BENCHMARK ROI CASE STUDY

Selecting Ideal Candidates

Replacing the 61 Wealth Managers scoring below average on the POPÿ with Ideal Wealth Managers is projected to increase the average annual net new money of this large global bank by $2,500,000,000

ROI: Average Annual Increase

$2.5B

As evidenced by the results of the study replacing the 61 low performers with the ICP would result in $2.5 billion annual increase in revenue.

Imagine the double impact: not only were they losing clients faster than they could acquire them, but the company was supporting these negative producers with full infrastructure costs. Almost all the Net New Business was coming from the top performers, who were essentially subsidizing their under-performing colleagues.

When you hire high Sales DNA, you're not just hiring a salesperson. You're hiring revenue. When you employ low Sales DNA, you're hiring an expense that masquerades as an investment.

The Characteristics of High Sales DNA

The number one competency of top sales performers is simple: they are responsible for their performance and accountable for their results. They are essentially impossible to manage or supervise in the traditional sense, which makes them unemployable in bureaucratic environments. However, they are incredibly fun and challenging to coach because they are committed to high daily activity levels, making them self-sufficient and maintenance-free.

These individuals rely on coaches not for basic supervision, but for growth, development, and help navigating administrative or political hurdles that might impede their progress. They're high achievers who are internally motivated, constantly seeking new challenges while keeping score and enjoying recognition from peers, coaches, and company leadership.

Attitudinally, they are upside thinkers who see opportunity where others see obstacles. They look for and focus on positives whereas underachievers tend to be downside thinkers and focus on negatives. Upside thinkers are passionate about their products and companies and genuinely believe they are helping their clients. This belief makes them effective closers and trustworthy in client relationships.

High Sales DNA individuals have strong work ethics and self-evaluate by taking control over the aspects of the sales process that are controllable. They create their own structure, when necessary, but will integrate with existing systems that facilitate their development without restricting innovation and evolution. Their self-confidence is based on conscious competence. They are aware of their strengths and can leverage those strengths when challenged or facing adversity. This is true resilience and grit.

These individuals also possess relatively high emotional intelligence and empathy. They have the IQ necessary to pass licensing requirements and acquire knowledge, enhance team performance, and generate profits for their companies. They tend to attract other top performers and maintain healthy, balanced lifestyles that prevent burnout while integrating family and personal commitments.

The Bottom Line

High-performing sales professionals represent only 17% of the population, making them incredibly valuable and more difficult to attract, hire, coach, and retain. They have options, they demand challenges and growth, and they won't tolerate mediocre environments or leadership. But they're worth every bit of effort and investment required to attract and develop them. The return on investment isn't just significant. It's transformational.

This book will show you how to find them, identify them, develop them, and keep them.

In sales, DNA isn't just an advantage. It's the foundation of high-performing teams and cultures.

> Sales DNA not only determines natural sales potential, but also defines the ideal environment for top performance.

CHAPTER 2

Sales Performance – Sales DNA: The Foundation (The Admission Ticket)

In chapter 1, we showed that identifying high-potential candidates early drives exceptional ROI, often adding hundreds of thousands to millions in revenue by replacing low-DNA performers with high-DNA talent. But what defines that potential? What separates the top 17% from the rest? The answer lies in understanding the science of sales performance, and the distinction between performance and results.

The Relationship Between Performance and Results

Top performers take responsibility for their performance and are accountable for their results. However, the difference between the two creates significant challenges for both self-managing individuals and coaches.

While there is a clear and strong relationship between performance and results, it is not 100%. Many components of performance are controllable by the individual, whereas results often depend on external factors such as the economy, company brand, or government regulations. Ultimately, the consumer controls the buying decision, adding further complexity as factors like competing needs, shifting priorities, and financial timing can all influence the outcome.

There is also frequently a delay between performance and results. For example, between the initiation of the sales process and the eventual sale. This delay can create confusion and even superstitious behavior. I have coached individuals who, months after a presentation, suddenly received an order and tried to explain the success with unrelated factors, such as wearing the same outfit or taking the same route to work, rather than recognizing the true performance-based causes. They lost perspective on what the controllable factors of their performance were that ultimately lead to the result. When a sales rep is in a slump, stops prospecting, or reduces effort, results may worsen. Unfortunately, if a coach focuses only on results, they may inadvertently reinforce poor habits by rewarding outcomes disconnected from performance. The result is a distorted feedback loop where the rep stops taking responsibility for performance, and both the rep and coach lose clarity about what truly drives success.

Responsible and Accountable

Ability to Delay Gratification — In the famous Marshmallow experiment by Walter Mischel (1971), a Stanford psychologist concluded that kids who could delay gratification and exercise self-control tended to have better life outcomes. Later research has subsequently questioned the predictive power of his findings, but the gap between sales performance and sales results definitely requires a sales performer to delay gratification and exercise self-control. A focus exclusively on results can confuse the relationship and the rep could give up the responsibility for performance. There is only one way to maximize results and that is by maximizing performance.

Top performers consistently evaluate their effectiveness based on controllable aspects of performance such as prospecting activity, presentation quality, and follow-up discipline, rather than the uncontrollable aspects of results. They remain accountable for results while reinforcing habits that they can directly influence.

After analyzing thousands of sales professionals across multiple industries and tracking their performance over time, we have found that sales success is neither random nor mysterious. It follows predictable patterns based on measurable personality traits and capabilities. By identifying and assessing these traits scientifically, organizations can turn sales hiring into a process of strategic precision rather than guesswork.

The Performance Equation

At Self-Management Group, our extensive research on more than 30,000,000 sales professionals has uncovered a consistent and predictable pattern behind top sales performance.

PERFORMANCE EQUATION

🫶 **TALENT**	🧠 **HABITS**	🕸 **OPPORTUNITY**

Inherent (DNA/Potential)	Trainable (Skills)	Attitude (Thoughts)	Effort (Behavior)	Career/Job	Work Environment

SALES DNA

CAN DO — WILL DO

PERFORMANCE — RETENTION

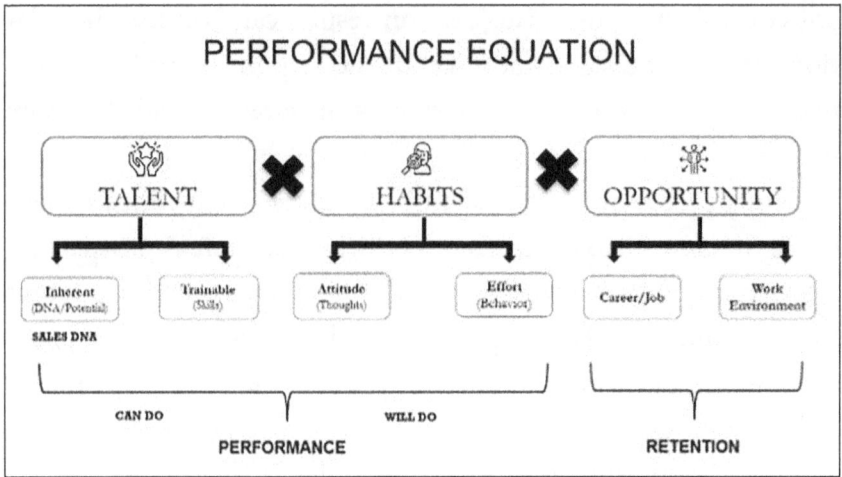

TALENT: The Inherent (Sales DNA/Potential) and The Trainable (Skills, Experience) "The CAN DO"

Inherent Talent (Untrainable):

The inherent or untrainable component of talent defines our potential. It evolves through life experiences but becomes largely fixed by our late teens to early twenties. The three major components of inherent talent are Personality, Emotional Intelligence (EQ), and Intelligence (IQ).

We have no control over the genetic foundations of our personality and very little responsibility for its formation. There is some debate, however, over how much control we have over our EQ. While EQ skills can be taught, the ability to consistently and effectively apply them is a more complex issue that will be explored later in this chapter. Similarly, IQ is largely genetic and how we apply our capacity to think, reason, and solve problems (Fluid Intelligence) will also be discussed later in this chapter.

Trainable Talent (Learnable):

Skills, competencies, and knowledge form the trainable side of talent. These can be developed and refined through education, coaching, and experience. Trainable talent is 100% controllable and 100% the responsibility of the individual—though its development is often supported by a coach or manager.

HABITS – Attitudes and Effort — "The WILL DO"

ATTITUDES (Habits of Thought)

The way we think is 100% controllable and 100% our own responsibility. Our attitudes are shaped throughout life by the influence and conditioning of parents, peers, teachers, coaches, and managers. By the time we begin our first career, most of these attitudes are well established.

It is interesting to note how people perceive sales careers and professionals. Despite offering unlimited earning potential and the opportunity to deliver real value to clients, sales is rarely a first career choice, or one that is encouraged.

EFFORT (Habits of Behavior)

All successful sales professionals share one key trait: a strong work ethic. It often develops early in life, shaped by lessons from parents and reinforced through first jobs or efforts to earn money for something special: a bike, a toy, or a goal. Work ethic is entirely within an individual's control and responsibility, becoming part of their Sales DNA by their late teens or early twenties.

OPPORTUNITY (Fit to Job/Career & Environment)

Fit is the primary predictor of both short-term and long-term retention.

Sales DNA not only determines natural sales potential but also defines the ideal environment for top performance. Achieving this alignment is a shared responsibility between the coach and the company. Fit to the coach requires that leaders understand their natural coaching style and adapt it to the individual's personality, motivations, and developmental needs. The coach ultimately controls the team, deciding who joins, who stays, and who succeeds. Fit to the corporate culture is equally vital. A high-performance culture must align with and support the sales force. The coach serves as the buffer between the corporate structure and the sales team, translating strategic goals into actionable performance behaviors. While high-Sales-DNA individuals can survive under any coach, on any team, and within any structure, they truly thrive when placed in the right environment through a strong fit. Top performers understand that their true job security lies in their marketability; organizations everywhere are constantly seeking them.

In summary, we have 100% control and responsibility over our trainable talent, attitudes, and work ethic. The only untrainable factor is our Sales DNA, which defines our innate potential and sets the ultimate ceiling for performance. This is why two salespeople with the same training, territory, and support can produce dramatically different results. One may consistently achieve 150% of quota year after year, while the other struggles to reach 80%, despite receiving identical investment and development opportunities.

This predictive model has been validated across industries from financial services to technology to retail. When any one factor is missing or significantly weak, overall performance declines sharply. For instance, a representative with high potential who fails to build skills, maintain effort, or demonstrate a positive attitude will fall short of both their current and ultimate potential.

While Sales DNA cannot be created, it can be developed and optimized through targeted training, coaching, and experience. Ultimately, the trainable factors transform potential into performance. Therefore, the foundation for accurately predicting performance begins with understanding an individual's potential.

In essence, predicting sales performance requires assessing this potential to help leaders evaluate the Return on Investment (ROI) in developing a given candidate, whether they are new to sales or already experienced. Simply put, average potential with maximum development will still produce average performance.

The Foundation: Sales DNA

Our research has identified three core personality traits that consistently predict long-term sales potential across all industries and sales roles. We call this your Sales DNA: the genetic code that determines your natural capacity for sales success.

Just as athletic performance depends on measurable physical qualities like speed, strength, and coordination, sales performance is driven by measurable psychological traits that predict success. These are the core elements of personality that tend to remain stable throughout a person's career. By understanding these underlying traits, we can accurately identify who is likely to thrive in sales and who may struggleregardless of experience or industry background.

The combination of three key traits represents the "Admission Ticket" or the minimum level of potential required to be part of the top 17% who truly can do the job. Much like in sports, without this Admission Ticket, it becomes extremely difficult to survive, let alone excel, in the competitive world of sales.

Enterprise Potential (EP): The #1 Predictor of Survival and Success

EP is the single strongest predictor of survival and long-term success because it reflects a person's natural ability to focus energy into prospecting and business development. Individuals with high EP are enterprising, competitive, goal-oriented, proactive, and self-initiating. They naturally channel their energy into productive, business-building activities.

EP is a source trait; a reflection of an individual's internal environment. In simple terms, it's in their guts or DNA. High-EP individuals take ownership of their inner world, which allows them to stay focused and productive even as the external environment changes around them.

High-EP performers are self-managers who take full responsibility for their daily Admission Ticket: the set of actions that drive consistent performance and results:

- Set and review daily goals upon waking.
- Identify controllable activities required to achieve those goals.
- Commit fully to executing those activities.

- Follow through and deliver by focusing energy on what they can control.
- Evaluate effectiveness and self-reinforce success to sustain motivation.
- Continuously improve by seeking feedback, coaching, and development resources.

This disciplined daily routine is what predicts not only survival but also sustained success.

Prospecting consistency and persistence: High EP individuals maintain prospecting activities even during busy periods or after successful closes. They understand that today's prospecting becomes next quarter's revenue, and they consistently allocate time to development regardless of their current workload.

Comfort with cold calling and networking: These salespeople don't experience the call reluctance that plagues many in the profession. They view cold calls as opportunities rather than obstacles, and they naturally gravitate toward networking events, trade shows, and other venues where they can meet potential prospects.

Ability to generate new business opportunities: Beyond just making calls, high EP individuals excel at identifying and creating opportunities. They naturally ask for referrals, identify expansion opportunities within existing accounts, and consistently uncover new market segments.

Resilience in the face of Resistance: Rejection doesn't discourage high EP salespeople as they self-evaluate on the controllable aspects of performance and reward themselves for keeping their commitments. They understand that external resistance and objections are not 100% controllable and continue to focus on their activity.

Initiative in seeking out potential clients: Rather than waiting for leads to be assigned, these individuals proactively research, identify, and pursue prospects. They're constantly building lists, researching companies, and finding creative ways to connect with decision makers.

High EP salespeople view prospecting as the lifeblood of their business, understanding intuitively that without a steady pipeline of new prospects, even the best relationship skills won't sustain long-term success. They are the ones making calls while others are finding excuses; they see a networking event as an opportunity rather than an obligation. They understand that prospecting isn't just about finding people to sell to. It's about building a foundation for financial security and professional growth.

These individuals often describe the prospecting process in favorable terms: exciting, challenging, energizing. They see each call as a puzzle to solve and each connection as a potential relationship to build. This positive association with prospecting activities creates a self-reinforcing cycle where success breeds more activity, which breeds more success.

Being proactive and taking initiative is an essential success factor in all levels and types of sales. High EP sales reps naturally ask for referrals, cross sell into enterprise clients and farm designated territories. Our top sales rep has lunch with his referral sources every 3 months to thank them for their referrals and of course ask for additional referrals. In addition, he reinforces each lead by offering our season tickets to the referral source for their local charities or for their corporate silent auctions. He views the closing of a sale of an enterprise client as the first step to earning the trust of the client by delivering on his commitments and earning the right to ask for referrals to cross sell within the company. Top residential real estate professionals when they sell a listing will naturally attempt to get referrals to other neighbors. We built our company on industry referrals. Early in my career we closed the #1 North American insurance company in terms of rolling 4-year retention, They were almost 3 times higher than the industry average. Opening the door to other top insurance companies was simply contacting sales leaders of other companies with the opening "You are probably wondering why the #1 company in North America in terms of 4 year retention is now using our POP assessment as part of their selection process." Of course, just about everyone was interested in booking a meeting as all top companies are searching for best practices and how they compare.

In summary, they are proactive and self-initiating. They don't wait for a coach or an external system to tell them what to do. They simply do it through their own initiative.

AP – Achievement Potential – AP is the #2 predictor of performance as it assesses energy, ambition, sense of urgency, motivational mix, closing style and risk taking. In our prediction model, Sales reps who prospect survive and those that prospect and close excel. High AP individuals have a lot of energy and a high sense of urgency. They are high achievers who expect results quickly and often have difficulty coping with the gap between performance and results. From a Motivational Mix perspective they are motivated primarily by Money and challenge. And secondarily by people, service and recognition and to a lesser degree by safety and security. This motivational mix creates a very interesting profile in terms of long-term success and closing style. The primary motivation of money and challenge explains the reason highly successful reps who are making a lot of money and financially successful continue to work hard. Once they become financially stable they remain challenge motivated and the external trappings of money are a way to keep score.

The high AP individual has a hard closing style. They view objections as a challenge rather than an obstacle and their high sense of urgency coupled with their need to achieve will result in pushing through objections. They have a balance of money/challenge and people service recognition but will not push through an objection and sacrifice the client relationship to simply get the sale. They are often viewed as persistently persistent but believe that once they have uncovered a need the best thing they can do is close the sale and look after the need of the client. Providing they believe in their product, it satisfies both their need to achieve and the client's need. If they are also high on people orientation they will be smiling as they close the sale. Soft closers are primarily motivated by people/service and recognition and secondarily by Money/challenge and score high average on AP. They would be described as persuasively persistent and would never sacrifice the client relationship to make a sale. High AP individuals are also more risk takers which indicates that would be a little more comfortable pushing through objections.

Very low AP individuals tend to be no closers as they are primarily motivated by safety and security and would seldom take the risk of damaging the relationship to push through an objection. In summary high EP and high AP individuals will prospect and close and achieve higher sales results quicker. A high EP and low AP individual will have high activity but potentially a closing problem so they might survive as order takers but take longer to achieve higher sales results. Coaches will need to be more patient with a low AP rep and focus on their commitment to product and the value to the client. EP dictates the level of results and AP dictates how quickly the results will occur. One very interesting profile we call the burnout result is the low EP and the high AP. In other words, a very high achiever with a lot of energy and drive but doesn't have the high EP to manage the energy and direct it into goals and results

In summary, AP predicts:

Closing consistency and effectiveness: High AP individuals are persistent in the sales process and effective at pushing through objections and staying focused on their sales tract. As effective closers they consistently convert opportunities into revenue.

High sense of urgency and need to achieve: When combined with a high EP score they set very high goals and have the energy to achieve results often and quickly. They like to keep score and thrive on internal competition.

Competitive drive and desire to win: High AP individuals want to be number one. They are driven to outperform previous results. This competitive fire sustains them through difficult periods and pushes them to meet expectations and set new performance standards.

Persistence through complex sales cycles: When deals stall or face obstacles, high AP salespeople don't give up easily. They find alternative approaches, involve additional stakeholders, and maintain momentum even when prospects go silent. They view obstacles as challenges to solve rather than reasons to quit.

Ability to ask for the business confidently: Perhaps most importantly, these individuals are comfortable when they are approaching the closing of a sale. They can ask for commitments, propose next steps, and request decisions without hesitation or apology. They understand that asking for the business is a service to qualified prospects.

High AP salespeople don't just build relationships. They advance them toward decisions and outcomes. They understand that being liked is nice, but being respected and looking after a client is best for both the client and the company. These individuals see objections as information rather than rejection, viewing resistance as a natural part of the decision-making process and a sign of client interest that brings them closer to understanding what is important to the client and a potential sale. Their internal drive for completion means they follow up consistently, address concerns directly, and maintain momentum throughout even the most extended sales cycles.

Independence Potential (IP)

IP is the #1 predictor of retention (primarily related to fit issues) and the #3 predictor of performance. It reflects how individuals relate to external structure, systems, feedback, and authority; essentially, how well they fit within an organizational environment. IP predicts coachability, the need for external direction, and how a person gives and receives feedback. It also influences team fit, whether someone thrives in a structured, collaborative environment or prefers autonomy and self-direction.

High-IP individuals are self-structuring and highly independent thinkers. They dislike unnecessary feedback, accept compliments but not flattery, and often interpret constructive criticism as criticism. They naturally prefer leadership roles such as team captain as opposed to being labelled a "follower."

They are often described as stubborn or difficult to manage because they resist being told what to do. However, they will follow systems and advice, but only if they believe those systems enhance or complement their own approach. When paired with a high Enterprising Potential (EP), this self-management ability makes them ideal for remote or entrepreneurial roles, such as developing new territories with minimal direct supervision. A lighthearted way to describe high-IP individuals is: "You can't tell them anything." They won't ask for directions even when lost. When a manager gives them instructions, they often respond (verbally or nonverbally) with, "I'm not doing that," or "You do it." As we will explore in the coaching section, this trait explains why great coaches spend most of their development time with top performers, using a "asking vs. telling" approach. These individuals respond far better to collaborative guidance than to directives.

When onboarding a new rep with a high IP, particularly in companies that require adherence to a strict structure or defined process, the coach's goal is to negotiate an agreement, not enforcement. A useful principle is: "You must first learn to do it our way to earn the right to do it your way." For instance, a company may require new sales reps to memorize a set script. High potential individuals with strong IP and EP scores experience higher turnover when forced to follow rigid, unnatural processes. To be effective, any sales process must feel authentic, not contrived. Top performers always personalize their approach using their own words, examples, and rhythm, while staying aligned with the underlying sales track. Thus, teaching a sales script is essential, but the best results come when individual adaptation is encouraged within the defined structure.

Obviously, if someone does not survive in the role, it will be considered a performance issue. The two main reasons top performers leave voluntarily are either lack of fit with their manager or compensation issues. Interestingly, "fit" is also the number one predictor of short-term performance problems, as early turnover is often rooted in a fit issue.

We typically clarify this by tracking the reasons for turnover. Involuntary turnover (when a coach terminates an individual) is usually tied to performance issues, most often linked to low EP (prospecting challenges) or low AP (closing challenges). Voluntary turnover, on the other hand, is often a fit issue, which may be triggered by either the individual or the coach.

We also find that coaches and companies tend to tolerate high performers longer than poor performers, making greater efforts to adjust the environment or coaching style to address fit challenges. However, this also depends on the organizational environment. For example, if the role requires someone to strictly follow a word-for-word script rather than adapt a sales track to their strengths, we recommend not to hire a high IP (Independence Potential) entrepreneurial type.

IP distinguishes intrapreneurs from entrepreneurs, as both groups typically have high EP and AP scores. An entrepreneur likes to create their own structure whereas intrapreneurs need a structure and system to follow. Some sales positions are perfect for entrepreneurial candidates who want to build their block of business and client base under the umbrella of an established brand or enterprise company. Startups and new franchises, for instance, tend to require entrepreneurial talent, whereas established organizations and mature franchises benefit more from candidates who follow defined structures and systems.

Finally, selling a sales career to an entrepreneur is very different from selling one to an intrapreneur, and understanding that distinction is key to improving both performance and retention.

Additional Supporting Traits

Beyond the core Sales DNA, several other traits influence sales effectiveness and help predict how someone will approach different aspects of the sales process:

CWC Comfort with Conflict — Handling objections, call reluctance and rejection

In most sales environments, there is the potential to experience the perception of rejection or negative feedback especially in competitive sales positions that have a daily demand for prospecting. On first contact the chances of encountering a negative or positive response from a new contact or prospect are determined by several factors outside the control of the sales professional. When approaching a new potential client the success of the initial contact leading to a sales presentation is dependent on external issues such as need for the product or service, life's circumstance, mood of the prospect, current financial situation, etc. Some training programs attempt to deal with this by saying you can expect 10 nos before a yes, so every no is a step closer to a yes. But it varies so it could be 20 nos to 1 yes today or 2 nos to 2 yeses tomorrow, Confusing and possibly de-motivational and leading to feelings of incompetence and call reluctance. The main cause of call reluctance is internalizing an objection or a no as a personal rejection rather than self-evaluating on reaching the prospect and doing the best introduction possible. In the sales presentation, there are always potential objections so CWC and AP combine to predict whether an individual will develop call reluctance or be resilient and push through objections and continue to do the best presentation to the next contact. Low CWC reps will feel rejected and allow that internal feeling to interfere with their effectiveness during the next contact. It is the "I guess you don't want to talk to me feeling."

Style Components of Sales DNA

Implicit in our discussion of the predictive power of source traits, substance not style predicts performance and retention. The biggest myth pertaining to top sales performers is that they are all extroverts and extremely outgoing. This is simply inaccurate. Top performers can be introverts and very technically oriented. Style predicts approach to clients and helps trainers and coaches maximize effectiveness. There are 2 fundamental style orientations: People Oriented (PO) and Analytical Oriented (AO).

People Oriented (PO):

High PO individuals are warm, friendly and enthusiastic. They develop new relationships quickly and are often viewed as the ideal sales candidate based exclusively on their PO. Interviewers immediately like them which can create the chemistry trap. In our research many recruiters and interviewers base their hiring decisions on likeability and stop asking tough questions once they like a candidate. Likeability can be a screening variable but should never be a selection factor. If you are a warm, friendly person you have probably been told that you should be in sales. If you can't prospect or close you will have no one to engage with and smile at. High PO reps will approach clients from a relationship perspective and be very effective at establishing immediate rapport with a new prospect. Low PO reps require more time to develop an interpersonal relationship with a new prospect.

Analytical Orientation (AO):

High AO individuals are factual, technical, and analytical. They enjoy learning and will often become subject matter experts and approach prospects as technically competent and can be viewed as introverted. They will require an agenda for their sales presentations and build trust through their competence. They can be overlooked by hiring managers if style is viewed as a major predictor of future sales performance. Low AO reps will only learn what is necessary to be effective whereas high AO enjoy learning even if there is no immediate application. A potential danger with extremely high AO reps is they might not feel comfortable prospecting and approaching new prospects until they believe they are product experts. As product experts they will develop Trust through their competence and enjoy educating the client. In our research, some of the best performers are low PO and high AO.

Great sales performers can be high PO or high AO or high on both. High PO individuals engage potential clients from an interpersonal perspective and establish the first level of trust through communality. If they are low AO they will bring along a product expert. Being aware of style will help trainers and coaches maximize individual style differences rather than assuming everyone learns and approaches clients from the same orientation.

Some are high on both PO and AO and adjust their style based on the perception of reading which approach will be best for a specific client.

Sales DNA in Action: Role-Specific Applications

Different types of sales roles require various combinations of these traits, and our POP™ (Predictor of Potential) assessment weights these traits based on the specific demands of each role. These weightings aren't arbitrary. They are based on analyzing thousands of top performers in each sales category to identify the trait combinations that consistently predict success.

Understanding these role-specific requirements helps organizations avoid the common mistake of assuming that a successful salesperson in one environment will automatically succeed in another. A top performer in relationship sales may struggle in competitive sales, not because they lack talent, but because their natural trait combination doesn't align with the new role's requirements.

In competitive sales environments (such as financial services, technology, and insurance), salespeople must generate their own opportunities in competitive markets where prospects have multiple alternatives and are often satisfied with their current solutions.

Enterprise Potential: 45% - Prospecting becomes the primary differentiator because they must create their own leads and lead generation strategies. Success requires consistently identifying and approaching new potential clients who may not even realize they need your solution.

Achievement Potential: 40% - Strong closing skills drive revenue because competitive sales often involves longer cycles, more complex decisions, and sophisticated prospects who will thoroughly evaluate alternatives before making commitments.

Independence Potential: 15% - While creativity matters, coachability ensures consistent execution of proven methodologies that have been refined through extensive testing and optimization.

Success in competitive sales is clear: if you prospect through daily activities, you will survive. If you prospect and close effectively, you will excel. If you fit with your coach and team while doing both, you will thrive and stay. This role demands the highest levels of both business development and closing ability because the rep must find and initiate the front end of the sales process and then be very effective at opening an opportunity and establishing a potential need with a new prospect.

In relationship sales environments (such as automotive dealerships, retail environments, and point of sale real estate), prospects often come to salespeople through marketing efforts, referrals, or because they have already decided to buy something. The primary challenge becomes converting interested prospects into actual sales and creating exceptional experiences that generate referrals and repeat business.

Enterprise Potential: 25% - While some prospecting matters, leads often come through established marketing channels, referrals from satisfied customers, or prospects who walk in with existing interest. The focus shifts from finding prospects to maximizing conversion rates.

Achievement Potential: 55% - Converting relationships and interest into actual sales becomes the key differentiator. This requires the ability to understand prospect needs, overcome objections, and effective closing approach and skills.

Independence Potential: 20% - Following proven processes becomes more important because relationship sales often involve standardized approaches, established pricing structures, and company-wide service standards that must be maintained consistently.

In relationship sales, success depends heavily on the ability to build trust quickly, understand what prospects want and convert trust into sales. The best relationship salespeople create experiences so positive that customers naturally refer friends and family, creating a self-sustaining cycle of new opportunities.

Key account sales involves long-term relationships with major clients where salespeople must balance account maintenance with growth initiatives and cross selling often navigating sophisticated organizational dynamics and multiple decision makers.

Enterprise Potential: 30% - Growing existing accounts requires initiative and entrepreneurial thinking to identify expansion opportunities, but the prospecting focus shifts from finding new companies to finding new opportunities within existing relationships.

Achievement Potential: 45% - Complex closes demand strong achievement potential because key account sales often involve large dollar amounts, long decision cycles, and multiple stakeholders who must all be influenced and aligned toward a decision.

Independence Potential: 25% - Strategic thinking and problem-solving require some independence, but successful key account managers must also work within corporate guidelines and collaborate with internal teams to deliver complex solutions.

Key account managers must master the delicate balance between maintaining existing relationships and pushing for growth, between providing excellent service and asking for additional business, and between acting independently and collaborating with internal teams.

The Role of Emotional Intelligence (EQ)

While Sales DNA provides the foundational capacity for sales success, Emotional Intelligence amplifies performance by helping salespeople navigate the complex human elements of selling effectively. EQ skills can significantly enhance the natural abilities indicated by Sales DNA. In some cases, high EQ can help individuals with moderate Sales DNA perform better than those with higher DNA but lower emotional intelligence.

Our comprehensive EQ assessment measures six critical dimensions that directly impact sales effectiveness. Unlike personality traits that remain relatively stable throughout someone's career, EQ skills can be developed and improved through focused training and practice, making them valuable areas for ongoing professional development. Our EQ assessment measures six critical dimensions. The first 4 involve self-awareness and understanding your own emotions and the last 2 focus on the awareness of others.

Self-Awareness (Mood Labeling and Monitoring) Mood Labeling and mood monitoring are self-awareness oriented and based on the premise that it is necessary to understand yourself before you can understand the impact you might have on others. Being aware of your emotions and mood would certainly help a sales rep understand how others might be perceiving him/her. How often an individual checks into monitoring their emotions can vary by situations but managing energy output is an important factor in maintaining a healthy mood and preventing burnout. Top sales professionals can accurately label their emotions and monitor their own emotional state when required by the situation.

Self-Control: The ability to manage impulses, emotions, and reactions under pressure, especially during challenging sales situations. This means staying calm when prospects are difficult and avoiding emotional reactions that could damage relationships or interfere with the sales process. Strong self-control allows a rep to respond strategically rather than react emotionally and is a mediating factor when predicting sales performance. Self control is particularly important in the sales presentation when approaching the closing of a sale. Sales reps often speed up their approach when nervous or approaching the close which creates uncertainty with a client if they notice the change in pace.

Managing Emotional Influences: The capacity to stay focused on necessary actions despite emotional challenges or distractions. This separates professionals who make calls even when they don't feel like it from those who let emotions interfere with their productivity. This ability relates strongly to the response from the feelings of rejection after a negative client reaction. For example, if a rep is making a series of calls to fulfil their activity Admission Ticket and a client indicates in a hostile manner they are not interested, the rep allows the call to negatively impact their next call. This would also increase the probability of a negative result on the next call. Repeated negative consequences of calls can create call reluctance.

Empathy: The ability to understand and respond appropriately to the emotions of others, including prospects, clients, and team members. This characteristic is essential for building genuine rapport and adapting to the feelings of others. There is a debate as to whether empathy can be trained. Empathetic skills can be trained but the debate is over the application of skills or natural empathy. For example, we can teach an individual to say,

" I understand how you feel." However, if it is not genuine it might be perceived as scripted rather than natural.

Social Judgment: The ability to make appropriate decisions in social and business situations based on reading the emotional and social cues of others. Empathy and social judgement are both required to be effective in the sales process. For example, a rep could have natural empathy and be aware of the emotional state of a client but have poor judgement and not know how to respond. The combination of empathy and judgement are essential for closing and determining when and how to close a sale. Many studies have demonstrated that we can train individuals to recognize the behavioral correlates of the emotional states of others but it is a complex process and varies across many factors such as gender and culture.

In summary, the 6 EQ components can help high Sales DNA individuals maximize their natural potential and be more effective in the sales process. The key insight is that while Sales DNA sets the foundation and ceiling for performance, EQ skills can improve the application of a sales rep's natural tendencies. Sales professionals who have natural EQ will respond quickly to EQ skills training and immediately be able to apply and benefit from the training. Natural EQ would help top sales performers move closer to their ultimate potential. EQ might be best described as being smart or street smart whereas IQ is being intelligent. As a former university lecturer, I met a number of professors who were extremely intelligent but not street smart. Also, a number of street smart sales professionals who were average IQ. As Daniel Goleman wrote in his book "'Emotional Intelligence: IQ gets you hired; EQ gets you promoted." Great sales professionals are aware of their feelings, control their feelings and are extremely good at understanding the feelings of others and judging when and how to close a sale.

The Intelligence Factor (IQ)

The only thing IQ reliably predicts is academic performance, such as grade point average. It has virtually no correlation with sales performance. IQ becomes relevant only in roles that involve demanding technical or licensing requirements where above-average intelligence is necessary.

Our research shows that a high school education with solid grades,or any college degree typically reflects sufficient intelligence for success in sales. Beyond this baseline, higher IQ does not translate into stronger sales results.

What does matter is fluid intelligence; the ability to apply one's intelligence effectively in dynamic, real-world situations. Fluid intelligence is closely linked to Sales DNA and Emotional Quotient (EQ), both of which are far stronger predictors of sales success.

One of our clients once shifted their hiring strategy to focus exclusively on MBAs and adopted a seminar-selling approach. The logic was that MBAs, being highly intelligent and business-savvy, would quickly gain credibility with a high-net-worth audience. The strategy failed almost immediately because no one on the team could actually fill the seminars with potential clients. Once again, this reinforces a key principle: Sales DNA is the foundation of any sales strategy and long-term success. Everything works better when it starts with the 17%.

The next chapter will explore the trainable aspects of talent and how to maximize potential built upon the untrainable foundation of Sales DNA. Individuals with high Sales DNA are naturally driven to seek out new resources, continuously improve their performance, and move closer to realizing their full potential.

"
There's a common fallacy in sales
and sports: "You have to lose in order
to learn how to win." The reality is
exactly the opposite: you need to win
to learn how to win.
"

CHAPTER 3

Trainable Talent – Knowledge, Skills, Experience

As discussed earlier, Performance = Talent × Habits.

The Talent predictor includes two equally important components: Sales DNA (the natural, hardwired traits) and Trainable Talent (the knowledge, skills, and experience) that can be developed.

Sales DNA determines the potential ceiling of performance, while Trainable Talent dictates how close a sales representative comes to reaching that ceiling. Without the natural Sales DNA, even the best training often yields limited results, making it an inefficient investment of time and resources.

In our team-building framework, which we will explore later, we refer to individuals who possess high DNA potential but fail to develop their skills and knowledge as Talent Traps. These people appear promising because of their innate ability, but their lack of continuous growth often goes unnoticed during hiring and throughout their career. As a result, they never fully realize their potential despite having the raw ingredients for success.

The second element of Talent, the CAN DO or trainable component, is where top performers distinguish themselves. High achievers are self-aware (Consciously Competent) and actively pursue growth through education, training, coaching, and experience. They also recognize their development needs (Consciously Incompetent) and use this awareness as the foundation for improvement.

While "potential" is an overused term, it remains vital to understand that potential alone is not enough. Many individuals have potential but lack the awareness of their strengths (Unconsciously Competent), the clarity on how to develop (Unconsciously Incompetent), or the willingness to invest the effort required for growth.

Top sales performers, on the other hand, operate with conscious competence—they know what they do well, apply it consistently, and deliberately leverage their strengths when challenged. This ability to repeatedly perform at their best is what transforms potential into sustained performance.

Continual Growth and Development

The greatest athletes of all time, Michael Jordan, Tom Brady, Wayne Gretzky, and Serena Williams, are perfect examples of continual growth and development. Despite already being among the best, they never stopped refining their craft. Debate often centers on whether they succeeded because they had more natural talent (DNA) or because they pushed themselves closer to their full potential through dedication, discipline, and constant improvement. The truth is, it was both. They possessed extraordinary natural ability and maximized it through relentless effort and commitment to personal development.

The beauty of Sales DNA is that, unlike athletics, the career path in sales can extend for decades. Age does not limit growth until much later in life, and even then, many sales professionals can maintain peak performance by leveraging technology, virtual assistants, and support systems to offset declines in physical energy.

Across all fields, a consistent pattern emerges: top performers are both Consciously Competent (CC) and Consciously Incompetent (CI). They are aware of their strengths and continue to build on them, but they are also aware of their weaknesses and actively work to improve them, unlocking their full learning potential.

By contrast:

The arrogant performer is CC but Unconsciously Incompetent (UI).They learn only from their successes and ignore their blind spots, limiting long-term growth.

The self-doubter is Unconsciously Competent (UC) and CI. Aware of weaknesses but blind to strengths, which slows progress and erodes confidence.

The disengaged performer is both UC and UI. They are unaware of both strengths and weaknesses, resulting in little or no growth potential. They are sometimes referred to as Silent Quitters.

Sustained excellence requires both awareness and humility— the willingness to keep learning, evolving, and investing in oneself, long after initial success has been achieved.

LEARNING POTENTIAL MODELS

	DESCRIPTION	Learning	Label
I Conscious Competence Conscious Incompetence	Learning from what we do well Learning from what we do not do well	FULL	SELF-CONFIDENT
II Conscious Competence Unconscious Incompetence	Learning solely from what we do	1/2	ARROGANT
III Unconscious Competence Conscious Incompetence	Learning solely from what we do not do well	1/2	SELF-DOUBTER
IV Unconscious	No Learning	0	DISENGAGED

This learning potential explains why two sales representatives with similar natural talent (Sales DNA) can have dramatically different career trajectories. The self-confident rep who is aware of both strengths and growth opportunities continues to develop and maximize potential, whereas the arrogant individual who only focuses on existing strengths, eventually plateaus when the market or role requirements evolve beyond their current skill set.

How We Learn

There are three primary pathways for developing trainable talent: Knowledge, Skills, and Experience. Each pathway requires different strategies and investments, but all three must work together to maximize potential.

Knowledge

Knowledge acquisition has become easier and more accessible than ever before. Several resources are available: digital books, online courses, seminars, podcasts, webinars, research papers, and professional journals. The challenge is no longer access to information but rather discernment, identifying which knowledge is most relevant and valuable for growth. Top performers are voracious consumers of knowledge but are also strategic about what they consume. They focus on knowledge that builds on their strengths or addresses specific growth opportunities rather than randomly consuming content.

A common mistake in knowledge development is taking an ipsative approach (yes/no) rather than a normative approach (rating on a scale). This is often the trouble with evaluating knowledge and skills during the selection and development process. For example, asking "Do you have sales experience?" is an ipsative question and provides limited useful information. A more effective (normative) approach would be to ask "How many years of sales experience do you have?" or better yet, "Rate your competence in consultative selling on a scale of 5 to 1 (excellent to poor) and provide specific examples of when you've applied these skills." The same principle applies to emerging technologies and tools. Asking "Are you familiar with ChatGPT?" is far less valuable than asking "How have you used AI to increase the efficiency and effectiveness of your sales process? Can you give some specific examples?"

The distinction between knowing about something and knowing how to apply it is critical. Many sales reps attend seminars, read books, and complete courses but never translate that knowledge into changed behavior or improved performance. Knowledge without application is simply trivia. Top performers not only acquire knowledge but immediately ask themselves, "How can I apply this to my current situation?" and "What is the one thing I can implement from this learning?" They treat knowledge acquisition as an investment that must generate a return through application.

Skills: Conscious Competence Building on Our Strengths

Skills development requires moving beyond knowledge into practice and application. Again, it's essential to take a normative not an ipsative approach when evaluating skills. Rather than asking "Can you handle objections?" (ipsative), the more valuable question is "Rate your competence in handling objections on a scale of 5 to 1, and describe your process for addressing the three most common objections you encounter" (normative). This approach provides much richer information about actual skill levels and identifies specific areas for development.

One of the most powerful concepts for skill development is what we call Compounding Effectiveness. This involves taking something we do well, breaking it down into component units, and developing a strategy to incrementally improve each component. The mathematics of compounding effectiveness is compelling. Consider a simple example with five components where each is rated at 1: $1 \times 1 \times 1 \times 1 \times 1 = 1$. Now, if we improve each component by just 10%:

1.1 x 1.1 x 1.1 x 1.1 x 1.1 = 1.61. A modest 10% improvement across all components yields a 61% improvement in overall effectiveness.

Let's apply this to a practical example using the skill of Business Development. Consider these five core components, each rated on a 5-to-1 scale (Excellent, Above Average, Average, Below Average, Poor):

Business Development Skill Components:
- Prospecting (sourcing prospects, natural market): 3
- Initial Interview (Script & fact find): 4
- Prepare Closing Interview (PPT and Marketing materials): 4
- Handling Objections & Closing sale: 3
- Obtaining referrals: 4

Current effectiveness: 3 x 4 x 4 x 3 x 4 = 576

Now, let's improve each area by just 10%: Improved effectiveness: 3.3 x 4.4 x 4.4 x 3.3 x 4.4 = 928

By improving each component by only 10%, overall effectiveness increases by 61%. This demonstrates the power of systematic, incremental improvement across all skill areas rather than attempting dramatic overhauls in one area.

We could further break down each of the five skill areas for even more granular development. For example, let's examine "Handling Objections & Closing ASale" in detail:

Handling Objections & Closing Sale Sub-components:
- Building rapport and establishing trust
- Following the script while remaining natural and conversational
- Active listening to understand the client's true concerns
- Trial closing to test readiness and identify remaining objections
- Addressing objections with empathy and evidence
- Final closing with proper timing and summarizing the value proposition

If a sales rep rates themselves a 3 overall in Handling Objections & Closing, they might discover they're actually a 4 in building rapport and listening, but only a 2 in trial closing and addressing objections. This granular awareness allows for targeted development rather than generic objection-handling training. The rep can focus their energy on the specific sub-skills that will yield the greatest improvement.

Another practical application of compounding effectiveness involves adding new capabilities to existing strengths. For example, a sales rep might be strong in all five business development components but recognizes that adding Al as a virtual assistant could enhance efficiency:

Sales Presentations

- CC (Current Strengths): Prospecting, Initial interview, Prepare Closing interview, Handling Objections, Obtaining referrals

- CI (Growth Opportunity): Al Virtual Assistant for research, personalization, follow-up automation, and CRM management

By maintaining excellence in core skills (CC) while adding technological leverage (CI), the sales rep compounds their effectiveness. They're not replacing their strengths but amplifying them through strategic addition of new capabilities.

The Rule of 72 provides additional perspective on the power of continuous improvement. With 10% annual compounded growth, output doubles every 7.2 years. This applies not just to investment portfolios or salaries but also to skill development. A sales rep who systematically improves their skills by 10% annually will double their effectiveness in just over seven years. Over a 20-year career, this compounds into extraordinary performance levels that far exceed what's possible through natural talent alone.

Conscious Incompetence: Learning a New Skill or Acquiring New Knowledge

While building strengths through Conscious Competence is essential, growth also requires developing new capabilities (moving into areas of Conscious Incompetence). Let's return to our business development example. If the rep adds a sixth component (using Al as a virtual assistant), their equation changes from 5 components to 6:

Current: $3 \times 4 \times 4 \times 3 \times 4 = 576$ Adding CI (starting at 1): $3 \times 4 \times 4 \times 3 \times 4 \times 1 = 576$

Initially, the new skill doesn't improve performance, it's neutral. But once developed: With Al improved to 1.5: $3 \times 4 \times 4 \times 3 \times 4 \times 1.5 = 864$

And with continued improvement across all six areas (10% each): 3.3 x 4.4 x 4.4 x 3.3 x 4.4 x 1.65 = 1,531

The willingness to acknowledge Conscious Incompetence and invest in developing new capabilities separates top performers from those who plateau. Many sales reps resist learning new skills because they feel incompetent during the learning process. They would rather stay in their comfort zone of Conscious Competence than endure the temporary discomfort of not being good at something. This resistance to Conscious Incompetence is one of the primary reasons talented individuals never reach their potential.

We could further break down each of the skill areas to create even more targeted development plans. For example, evaluating the sales presentation script in terms of:

- Building rapport and creating emotional connection
- Defining perceived need through strategic questioning
- Following the script structure while remaining flexible
- Listening actively to verbal and non-verbal client cues
- Trial closing at appropriate moments throughout the presentation
- Handling objections with confidence and empathy
- Final closing with proper timing
- Summarizing the sales process and next steps

Each of these sub-skills can be rated, practiced, and improved independently, yet they compound together to create an exceptional sales presentation capability.

Learning Through Experience

There's a common fallacy in sales and sports: "You have to lose in order to learn how to win." The reality is exactly the opposite you need to win to learn how to win. Success builds character, not failure. Success and winning are very different concepts, though they're often confused. Success is playing up to your potential (performance), which is internal and controllable. Winning is the outcome, which is external and often dependent on factors beyond our control. As we discussed in the attitude chapter, focusing on controllables (success) rather than uncontrollables (winning) is a characteristic of top performers and critical for long-term development.

As a coach and consultant working with top performers, the advice is always the same: Maximum performance comes from doing what you do well as often as possible (CC). Minimum performance results from focusing only on what you don't do well (UC). On game day, you can't work on weaknesses. Winning requires executing strengths and exploiting the weaknesses of your opponent. The ideal strategy for winning in sports is the same as winning in business: Execute your strengths and exploit the weaknesses of your competition.

For example, our competitive advantage is that we predict performance and retention. We have over four decades and thousands of studies demonstrating our predictive power, with millions of assessments proving the ROI associated with using our products. Our competitors may claim they can predict performance, but they lack the research, validation, and real-world experience to substantiate those claims. This creates a strategic opportunity during the sales conversation: present our proven data, analytics, and insights, then invite prospects to compare our evidence with our competitors and ask them to provide similar proof. The most effective strategy is to make competitors play on your terms, where you are strongest and they are weakest, giving you the greatest advantage to not just succeed, but win.

Learning through experience tends to help us improve by learning how to apply our knowledge, our hard skills and soft skills in real-world situations. However, experience alone doesn't guarantee learning. It's the reflection on and analysis of experience that drives growth. Two sales reps can have the same five years of experience, but one has truly learned and grown while the other has simply repeated one year of experience five times.

The Interaction of Trainable Talent with DNA

In the previous chapter we discussed whether EQ and IQ can be trained or if they are hardwired. The answer reveals the important interaction between DNA potential and trainable talent.

Fluid Intelligence: Experience can help us learn how to use our intelligence more effectively, providing we continually assess and evaluate our effectiveness. This can sometimes be confused with EQ, as we learn to apply our IQ in more sophisticated ways. If we have the natural aptitude of intelligence, we can then learn through experience how to maximize what we have but training doesn't actually change the DNA aspects of intelligence. This is the interaction effect of the two types of talent and demonstrates the CAN DO aspect of the performance equation. Learning and experience help us maximize our potential, not increase it or fundamentally change it. The higher the IQ, the quicker we learn and maximize fluid intelligence. A sales rep with high natural intelligence learns from fewer examples, recognizes patterns more quickly, and adapts strategies faster than someone with lower natural intelligence, even if both receive identical training.

Emotional Intelligence (EQ): Similar to IQ, we can learn and develop skills and experiences that maximize several aspects of our EQ. For example, consider empathy. We can teach empathetic skills like saying "I understand how you feel" or mirroring body language, but these techniques sound more genuine with individuals who have natural empathy. The words and behaviors can seem unbelievable and forced for individuals who do not have natural empathy. It's the difference between a rehearsed script and authentic connection.

Also, we can study and be taught the verbal and non-verbal behavioral cues associated with various emotional states of others, the slight tension around the eyes that signals concern, the shift in posture that indicates discomfort, the change in tone that reveals excitement. However, we still need the natural ability to accurately judge what to do with this information in real time. Reading the signals is one thing; knowing how to respond appropriately is another.

We can also be taught strategies to control our own emotional states. For example, counting to ten before we react, or using deep breathing techniques to manage stress. A particularly effective strategy is recognizing the level of our emotional state and consciously moving from the emotional side of the brain to the factual side. I call this technique "SO-ing."

Here's a driving example that illustrates this principle. I live six minutes in normal traffic from my office. (NOTE: Traffic is a major stress producer for many people, which makes it an excellent opportunity to practice emotional management.) Let's say I'm driving to work behind a vehicle going slightly slower than the speed limit. I have two choices in how I respond:

Emotional Response: "Can you believe it? Where did this person learn to drive? They probably don't have a license! This is ridiculous! Now I'm going to be late!"

Factual Response (SO-ing): "SO, what is the actual consequence of driving slightly below the speed limit? I will arrive at work 30 seconds later than normal."

By asking "SO what?" I move from emotional to factual. The technique forces me to evaluate the actual impact rather than the perceived injustice. Thirty seconds is inconsequential, and recognizing this fact immediately dissipates the emotional reaction. This is a trainable skill that leverages whatever natural emotional intelligence we possess, but someone with high natural EQ will find this technique easier to master and apply consistently.

We can also learn to control the emotional states of others by strategically moving them from the factual to the emotional or from the emotional to the factual, depending on what the situation requires. This is often a critical component of the sales process. For example, exposing a need can create anxiety, and the solution to reducing that anxiety is to buy the product. We tend to buy based on both emotion and facts, and skilled sales professionals understand how to balance both elements throughout the sales process.

Consider this example from the 2013 flood in Toronto, ON. Cars were floating down the highway, basements were flooded, sewers were overwhelmed and backed up, and there was loss of power. The damage included ruined carpets, furniture, and drywall in thousands of homes. My wife immediately wanted a backwater valve to prevent sewer backup, a natural gas generator to power the whole house (our battery-operated sump pump had run out of power), a new high-capacity sump pump, and awnings to direct rainfall away from doors and windows. These were easy sales based on emotions, fear, anxiety, and the visceral memory of the crisis. There was a sense of urgency and heightened emotional state that shortened the typical decision-making process.

The professional sales reps sensed the emotional state and were very effective at shortening the sales process (High EQ). They acknowledged the stress we'd experienced, validated our concerns, and quickly moved to solutions. The inexperienced reps, however, went through their standard presentation, which was annoying to my wife who had already bought emotionally and was only interested in how much it would cost and when they could install it. She didn't need to be educated about why she needed these solutions, she'd just lived through the reason. The inexperienced reps failed to read her emotional state and adjust their approach accordingly.

This example demonstrates that while EQ skills can be trained, natural EQ makes the application seamless and authentic. The experienced reps didn't follow a script for "handling anxious customers" they genuinely sensed the emotional state and responded appropriately.

Connecting the Dots on Learning Soft Skills

Let's connect some dots on learning soft skills through this comprehensive example. As a consumer, think of the sales process if you have actually known or experienced a sales professional who possesses all the following qualities:

- High Achievement Potential (AP) and passionate belief in their product
- High Emotional Intelligence (EQ) — empathetic, warm, friendly, emotionally in control
- Strong Communication with Customers (PO) — listens actively to you
- Handles your objections with confidence and empathy (CWC)
- Is aware of your emotional states throughout the interaction (EQ)
- Comforts you and reduces your anxiety over uncovering a need (EQ)
- Closes the sale to reduce your anxiety and provide a value-added service or product to make your life better (AP)

This is the gold standard of sales performance. It represents the complete integration of DNA talent (AP, PO, EQ, CWC) with developed skills (listening, objection handling, closing) and experience (reading emotional states, timing, knowing when to move forward). You can train someone with high DNA in these skills and they will become exceptional. You can train someone with low DNA in these same skills and they will improve but likely never reach the same level of natural effectiveness and authentic connection.

Learning Experiences Related to Trainable Talent

One of the most interesting aspects of early learning that indirectly impacts the Talent component of performance is that we inherit the consequences of the influences of parents, teachers, coaches, trainers, and managers. In other words, previous experiences shape how individuals approach development, and these learned patterns can either accelerate or inhibit growth.

For example, natural athletic talent can be a blessing or a curse depending upon previous experiences for both coaches and individuals. For the individual, they might achieve and win based exclusively on natural talent and never learn to work hard or understand the importance of continual growth and development. They often experience early success in terms of winning, but as they move up into higher levels of competition where many of the athletes have similar natural talent but have also learned the importance of hard work and continual growth, they begin to experience failure and losing. This often explains the high dropout rates around puberty, when competition becomes more intense and natural talent alone is no longer sufficient.

I have a friend and we were both good (not great) natural athletes who won many competitions in the elementary grades and early high school. We then played competitive hockey outside of the educational system, and he dropped out of competitive hockey to play rec league. He was at least the same and possibly higher in natural ability than me, but he never worked hard. He had never been taught that hard work was necessary because his early success came too easily. Basically, we were both winning and being reinforced for results, but my dad and my initial coaches focused on and reinforced both results AND the importance of working hard with a good attitude. I learned that a strong work ethic is very important for success and is a life skill that prepares us for all future goals that we pursue. He learned that talent alone should be sufficient, and when it wasn't, he concluded the activity wasn't worth pursuing.

The IQ Example

In terms of IQ, I had a friend who was a member of Mensa and in school always got excellent grades (better than mine) but never studied. I would be up in my room studying for exams and he would knock on my door and attempt to get me to avoid studying for some competing activity. We both graduated from high school and went to the same university, but he flunked out and never got a degree. He was being reinforced by teachers and parents exclusively by looking at results and not the work ethic. His career path has been a reflection of his early experiences. He has had several jobs but gets bored and is either fired or voluntarily leaves. He gets hired again because of his intelligence, but he never progresses in a career path because he never learned to apply sustained effort or to work through challenges. When things got difficult, he had no reference point for perseverance because everything had always come easily.

This also explains the high dropout rates in early university years, as some students haven't learned good study and work habits and/or have been successful because of natural talent (IQ) without developing the discipline required for sustained academic achievement. University represents a step up change in difficulty, suddenly everyone in the class has high IQ, and those who never learned to study are at a significant disadvantage despite their natural intelligence.

Society's Role in Reinforcing Mediocrity

Our work with teachers shows that they often spend more time and resources on underachieving students or those with behavioral challenges than on students who are motivated and eager to learn. The self-directed, consciously competent learners, those most capable of growth, tend to receive the least attention simply because they don't demand it. This results in an unintended system where the most vocal or problematic students get support, while the high-potential learners who could thrive with added challenge and mentorship are left to develop on their own.

Society also rewards mediocrity over merit by giving participation trophies and ignoring hard-earned success. We've moved toward a system that celebrates showing up rather than excelling, which sends a dangerous message to developing talent. Everyone feels good in the short term, but no one learns the connection between effort, excellence, and achievement. The message becomes "your effort doesn't matter" rather than "your effort determines your outcomes."

These societal and educational experiences create the context in which individuals develop their relationship with growth and learning. Some individuals emerge from these systems with strong self-directed learning habits despite the environment. Others absorb the message that effort is optional and that talent alone should be sufficient. These learned patterns become deeply ingrained and often determine whether someone maximizes their potential or becomes a Talent Trap.

Talent Traps and Golden Eagles

In future chapters we will discuss how to identify and coach Talent Traps (high talent, poor habits) and Golden Eagles (high talent and good habits). The distinction is critical for resource allocation. Coaching a Golden Eagle is tremendously rewarding, they absorb every insight, apply every technique, and continuously improve. Coaching a Talent Trap is frustrating and often futile despite having the DNA for success, their learned patterns of avoiding discomfort and expecting results without effort create a ceiling on their performance that's difficult to break through without their willingness to change.

The tragedy of Talent Traps is that they often don't recognize they are Talent Traps. They attribute their early successes to their natural abilities and their later plateaus to external factors such as the market changed, the company's products aren't competitive, the compensation plan doesn't motivate them, the manager doesn't support them. They never recognize that the real issue is their unwillingness to invest in continual growth and development.

Summary: The Two Aspects of Talent

In summary, the Talent component (CAN DO) has two aspects:

1. **DNA Potential:** The natural, hardwired abilities we're born with
2. **Trainable Talent:** The learnable knowledge, skills, and experience we develop

The only way to maximize potential is through continual growth and development of soft skills, knowledge, and experience. If we stop growing, we never reach our potential. The environment continues to evolve, competition continues to improve, and markets continue to change—standing still is actually falling behind.

Interestingly, DNA Potential is 0% controllable, we are born with it. However, it is 100% the responsibility of the individual to become CC and aware of their potential, and to learn how to leverage their DNA through the development of trainable talent.

Trainable Talent is 100% controllable and 100% the responsibility of the individual. However, early experiences can confuse us, as life experiences sometimes take away our sense of responsibility and we become dependent on outside factors rather than on factors we control. As a result, we give up responsibility for our future performance and success in our academic pursuits and careers. We develop what psychologists call an external locus of control, believing that our outcomes are determined by luck, other people, or circumstances beyond our control rather than by our own efforts and choices.

Coaches and managers can sometimes burn out by taking responsibility for performance factors that they have no control over. They cannot control whether someone has DNA potential, and they cannot force someone to take responsibility for their own development. What they can control is providing the environment, resources, and feedback for growth, but the individual must choose to use them.

The Foundation: Potential Becomes Performance

The underlying foundation for predicting future performance is set by our potential. It is only through effective training, coaching, and experience that potential becomes performance. Therefore, by training skills and competencies and gaining experience, we can unlock our potential and subsequently our performance. Without development of trainable talent, DNA potential remains dormant, impressive on paper but never realized in actual results.

Through organizational strategies such as 360-degree feedback assessments, behavioral interviews, and structured performance reviews, we can assess current skills and competencies. Only with these insights can we then create targeted development plans to maximize potential and performance. Assessment without development is merely interesting information. Development without assessment is random and inefficient. The two must work together, accurate assessment of both DNA potential and current skill levels, followed by strategic development focused on the highest-leverage growth opportunities.

The 17% Principle

In any population, the majority,66%, falls in the average category. This is a statistical reality that applies to sales talent just as it applies to any other human characteristic. Another 17% falls below average, and 17% falls above average. This normal distribution is consistent across virtually every measurement of human capability.

Therefore, unless the Talent Acquisition (TA) process prioritizes potential through valid assessment, sales talent will be randomly distributed in the normal population. No matter how many resources are invested in individuals with average potential, the performance will be at best average or mediocre. Our research shows that the biggest waste of resources stems from attempting to develop individuals who simply do not have the potential to perform at the highest level. Individuals who look acceptable on the surface but lack the DNA potential to reach top performance levels, regardless of how much training and coaching they receive.

The mathematics are clear and unforgiving:

high potential = high performance
low potential = low performance

Investing the same resources in low potential individuals as high potential individuals produces dramatically different returns on investment. A company might spend $50,000 training and coaching a low potential rep and get them to average performance. That same $50,000 invested in a high potential rep might develop them into a top performer who generates 3-4 times the revenue.

The earlier that potential can be identified, the earlier we can focus resources on the 17% rather than the 83%. Most companies have been forced to filter through 83% rather than focusing on the 17%, leading to hiring a high number of average potential candidates. As a result, these candidates are given to trainers and coaches, forcing the trainers and coaches to invest substantial resources for average to marginal returns. The trainers and coaches become frustrated because they're doing everything right. Their training programs are excellent; their coaching is skillful, but the results are mediocre because they're working with mediocre potential.

The Training Paradox

In our consulting experiences, the biggest waste of resources and money is investing in individuals who have lower levels of Sales DNA (the 83%) and expecting high performance. As a result, companies end up training and developing average performers. All our clients are very good at developing the trainable talent, they have excellent training programs, skilled coaches, and sophisticated development systems. They become confused when the training doesn't necessarily result in high performance for all the candidates. They conclude that their training must be inadequate or their coaches need more development, when the real issue is that they are training people who lack the DNA potential to excel.

I once asked the President of a large financial services company why he continues to train and invest in all the sales candidates when only about half benefit from the training and achieve high performance.

He said, "Because we don't know who the ones are who have the potential to benefit from the training, apply the training, and end up being high performers. So we train everyone the same and hope for the best."

This is an enormously expensive hope. It means 50% of training resources are essentially wasted or at best, producing minimal returns. Valid assessment of DNA potential before training would allow this company to focus resources on the 50% who can benefit and achieve top performance, while screening out or redirecting the 50% who cannot.

The Three Components of Performance

One problem is that organizations often look only at the Talent aspect of predicting performance, and we all know as coaches that you can't win without talent. However, not all Talent issues are trainable. Most organizations treat every performance problem as a CAN DO trainable solution when it is more often a WILL DO issue (attitudes and effort) or a FIT issue (match between the individual and the role, market, or company). These are the other components of the Performance equation that we'll discuss in subsequent chapters.

Companies often get consumed with predicting sales performance, because not all high potential Sales DNA individuals perform up to their potential. Sometimes the issue is that they don't take responsibility for growth, they never invest in developing their potential. Sometimes it is a WILL DO issue, they have the natural talent and the skills but lack the work ethic or have destructive attitudes. Sometimes it's a FIT issue, they have both the talent and the habits but they're in the wrong role, with the wrong coach, or working for the wrong company.

Conversely, sometimes low potential Sales DNA individuals perform well on a short-term basis through a strong natural market (they happen to know many people who need the product), through a few lottery sales (random luck), or because the coach invests unlimited resources attempting to prove the Sales DNA assessment inaccurate. These situations can create false confidence in average performers and lead to poor strategic decisions about resource allocation.

The Path Forward

To predict sales performance, it is necessary to be able to assess the Talent (both DNA and Trainable), the Habits (both Attitudes and Effort), and the FIT (match between individual and opportunity), and then leverage all three components through ongoing coaching, growth and development. Assessment alone is insufficient. Development alone is inefficient without assessment. The two must work together strategically.

The remainder of this book will discuss how to maximize the Sales DNA potential of the 17%, how to identify them, how to develop their trainable talent efficiently, how to coach their attitudes and effort effectively, and how to ensure proper fit between their capabilities and their opportunities. Because, if we get the 17% right, if we identify them early, invest in them strategically, and retain them long-term, everything else in the sales organization becomes easier. They require less coaching to achieve more results. They respond faster to training. They take ownership of their own development. They become the foundation of a high-performance sales culture that attracts other top performers.

The goal is not to abandon the other 83%, they may be perfectly adequate performers in appropriate roles. The goal is to stop treating 83% as if they were the 17%, to stop investing top-tier resources in average potential, and to start making strategic distinctions that align investment with capability. This is not elitism; it's efficiency. It's the difference between hoping for high performance and systematically creating it.

> Another complicating factor for hiring managers and coaches is that good attitudes don't necessarily predict good performance, but bad attitudes definitely negatively impact performance.

CHAPTER 4

Attitudinal Habits – The "WILL DO"

As we discussed previously Performance = Talent x Habits. The Habit predictor contains 2 equally important aspects: Attitudes (Habits of Thought) and Effort (Habits of Behavior). The Talent component predicts CAN a sales rep do the job whereas the Habit component predicts WILL they do the job. Obviously if a representative does not have the Sales DNA or the "CAN DO" component, the "WILL DO" becomes irrelevant. In our team building model that will be discussed in a later chapter, we refer to representatives who have the potential but lack the work ethic or have bad attitudes as Talent Traps. Talent traps are the major challenge for hiring top potential candidates and for creating a high performance sales team. Talent traps look good on paper but the work ethic is often overlooked during the selection process as it requires hiring managers to focus extensively on the effort history and the attitudinal habits of a candidate through a structured interview. Talent traps are then hired and passed on to the coach for growth and development and integration into an existing sales team. Almost all coaches have the experience and knowledge to develop the Talent but often struggle in dealing with effort or attitudinal issues. The main reason is that attitudes and effort are 100% controllable and 100% the responsibility of the individual sales rep. In our self-management training programs, coaches often share during the sessions that attitude management at both the individual and coaching levels is one of the most challenging aspects of attempting to maximize performance and change behaviors, especially dealing with agents who don't work hard and don't keep their commitments to daily sales activities.

Another complicating factor for hiring managers and coaches is that good attitudes don't necessarily predict good performance but bad attitudes definitely negatively impact performance and often predict poor performance. As a result during the selection process, lazy candidates with a good attitude especially if it is accompanied by a high people oriented score, can create the Chemistry Trap and the candidate is rated highly because they are warm, friendly and enthusiastic and the hiring manager likes them. Liking someone is a nice but non-essential aspect of a predictive selection process that must focus on can they and will they perform on the job.

The habit patterns of both attitude and effort are often referred to as character. Sales reps with positive attitudes and who work hard are often referred to as having character. Generally, these 2 habit patterns are almost fully developed through all the previous reinforcement and development strategies of parents, teachers, coaches, peer groups, and professors by late teens or early 20s when an individual enters the workforce or begins their first career. One of my coaches always searched for mind vitamins as he believed just as we have vitamins for the body we also need vitamins for the mind. One of my favorites occurred in training camp after a very successful season. He wrote on the white board at training camp, "Talent may get you to the top but it takes Character to keep you there." The company and all the employees are inheriting the character and habit patterns both good and bad. The remainder of this chapter will focus on attitudes and attitude management.

A consistent finding is top performers as opposed to poor performers are upside thinkers and have a habit of looking for positives whereas poor performers are downside thinkers and are habitually looking for negatives. An upside thinker will look for positives in all aspects of their life: career, company, manager, coach, associates, and team whereas poor performers will look for negatives. An upside thinker will go into a work environment and be looking for all the things that are positive whereas the downside thinker will be looking for all the negatives. It is easy for a coach or recruiter to determine the habit pattern by simply asking a few open-ended questions, such as "What do you think of your last or current coach?" The upside thinker will start with positives before mentioning any negatives usually in about a 5:1 ratio of positives to negatives. The opposite is true of the downside thinker; they will start with negatives before mentioning a positive. It is interesting the effect of these 2 types of thinkers on other team members. Negative thinkers tend to be lightning rods of negativity. Misery loves company. I am certain our readers have had the downside thinker in their office who has attracted other negative thinkers. They are usually poor performers who attract other poor performers, and when they meet, they are discussing the reasons they are not performing well and blaming the coach, the company's marketing strategy, the products, the markets. They blame external factors and give up responsibility for the aspects of performance that are 100% within their control and 100% their responsibility. We could write a long book on creative ways of failing and the excuses we have heard for poor performers not performing well. The opposite is true of upside thinkers and top performers. They are focused on what is working well, the positives of the company, the products, the coach, and ways of getting better again in a 5:1 ratio. Changing downside thinkers to upside thinking is a major challenge typical of changing any negative habit and replacing it with a competing positive habit. Even trained therapists and psychologists require time and ongoing sessions to change ingrained negative attitudes.

The Power of Expectations

One of the most powerful Principles of Psychology is the principle of expectations. Whatever we expect about the performance of ourselves or of others will probably happen

If you think you can OR think you Can't. You are Correct.

From dissonance theory we know the ideal motivational gap between expectations and performance is 25%. Ideal motivation occurs when the gap between actual performance and expectations or sales targets is 25%. If the gap is significantly greater than 25% it appears unattainable and individuals become frustrated and if too great give up trying. As we move closer to the target or expectation our motivation begins to decrease unless a new target or expectation is established. Once the target is reached the motivation disappears unless the activity becomes the target. Establishing sales and activity targets it is essential for a coach to ask rather than tell. Telling results is compliance whereas asking for results is commitment. It is also important to realize that an individual's public targets are about 25% lower than their private targets. Goal setting and expectations start with commitment and move forward to results. Compliance starts with results and moves backward to commitment. Commitment is the price that someone is willing to pay in terms of activity and effort. Everyone wants external rewards, and the question is the price they are willing to pay. In one of our self-management training sessions, we were discussing dissonance theory and setting activity levels. One of the experienced coaches presented a situation she had with a new sales rep who was previously a stockbroker. When she asked him how many dials he was going to make every day, he responded 100. She asked the group what they would have done. One inexperienced coach said I would tell him he doesn't have to do that many with us because it is impossible and to lower his expectation so he wouldn't become frustrated as around 10 a day is our beginning standard. The coach said I let him try it as I was curious what would happen. The next day she asked him "how the calls went" and he said "I only did 50 and ran out of time." So she said "how many calls are you planning on doing tomorrow." He said "I think I can commit to at least 25 calls per day" and that became his daily activity level which was well above the 10 calls she was going to set for him.

Stereotypes are a major demonstration of the power of expectations. If you believe a certain group has a specific personality trait, you will look for attitudes and behaviors that reinforce what you believe. Both good and bad. For example, in sales, many people have a negative stereotype of sales professionals, which is often based on their experiences with a specific group or type of sales. This is particularly true for sales reps who are in a one interview close situation and are often required to be assertive and possibly aggressive hard closers such as Florida land sales, door to door sales and telephone solicitors. Based on one experience, people generalize to all types of sales. When I was in college and had very little money, my now wife and I would drive to Florida for our vacation. On the beach, there were always students offering a free dinner if you would attend a land sale presentation. It would be our best meal of the vacation and we would do 2-3 every vacation. During dinner there was a sales presentation about the value of purchasing Florida land. After the dinner there would be one sales rep at each table who would approach each couple about their interest level and comments. They were very aggressive hard closers and light on relationship building. One night, we indicated we didn't have any money to buy a property but thanked him for the dinner and presentation. He jumped up took off his shoe and started banging it on the table telling all at our table that we were missing a tremendous investment opportunity (high belief in product). He then said "if you were interested which of the properties would you buy." We said lot #45. So he yells loud enough for the whole room to hear "hold property 45." 2 couples at our table signed agreements. Years later we bought a Florida condo from an amazing Sales rep who was assertive and persistently persuasive who follows up every year to see how we are doing and how we are enjoying the condo. She also asks for referrals. As we discussed in the Sales DNA section, some sales reps are hard closers and others are soft closers, and both types of closers are prevalent in most types of sales environments. However, it is human nature to generalize from experiences to label specific groups which can become stereotypes.

In sports if a player gets labelled as having a bad attitude it often follows them throughout their career. In education, in their research on 'Pygmalion in the Classroom' conducted by Robert Rosenthal and Lenore Jacobson demonstrated that teachers' expectations of students' performance impacted students actual academic performance. It has been demonstrated in many studies that once a student is labelled as a problem student or a brilliant student that label follows the student throughout most of their academic career. It is passed on from teacher to teacher. It is interesting that once anyone develops an attitudinal reputation it follows them throughout their career and others who are aware of the reputation look for the external manifestations of the behaviors and attitudes to support the reputation. We then live up or down to our reputation.

Expectations Dictate Performance and Self-Confidence Dictates Expectations

SELF-CONFIDENCE
THE FOUNDATION FOR RESULTS

RESULTS

↑

PERFORMANCE

↑

EXPECTATIONS

↑

SELF-CONFIDENCE

↑

CONSCIOUS COMPETENCE

The #1 predictor of Expectations is Self-Confidence (SC) and the foundation of SC is Conscious Competence. The ONLY long-term motivator of human performance is Conscious Competence. If we feel that we do something well it becomes self-reinforcing.

For example with learning disability children being taught to write a specific letter. The teacher initially reinforced the student with Smarties each time they successfully completed the letter BUT once the student learned to complete the letter it became a habit and no longer required the external reinforcement. It was self-reinforcing and became a sense of achievement and personal success. Far more powerful than a Smartie. This will be a theme throughout the habits portion of this book. To make habits habitual requires self-reinforcement and is a characteristic of all top performers and self-managers. They don't rely on external factors for their motivation but are internally motivated.

The more self-aware and CC the higher the levels of Self Confidence. The higher the levels of Self Confidence the higher our expectations. The higher our expectations the higher our performance. From Dissonance theory, we know that the ideal motivational gap between Expectations and performance is 25%. As mentioned previously, when the gap is 25%, we are motivated to close the gap. If the gap is greater than 25% it becomes frustrating and unattainable and de-motivating and we quit trying. That is the reason we need to constantly grow as our performance increases to maintain the gap between performance and expectations and continue to be motivated. Conscious Competence must be based on reality and cannot be simply Positive Mental Attitude.

A characteristic habit of top performers is they are compulsive achievers and put themselves in situations to achieve. This was demonstrated in the classic Ring Toss experiment given to achievers and to nonachievers. Without directions from the experimenter, the groups were tasked with learning how to throw the ring on a round peg. The compulsive achievers started close to the peg and once they became comfortable and successful with tossing the ring on the peg, they moved a little farther away. If they became unsuccessful they moved back to the previous position. They continued for a long period of time and only stopped when they felt outside their ability to be successful at the task. In terms of dissonance theory, they were internally motivated to continue the task until the gap between their ability and performance became greater than 25%. The underachievers moved a long distance away from the peg and simply tossed the ring as far as possible and were very seldom successful. They didn't expect to achieve and quickly became uninterested in the task. It is the old finding: Success breeds success.

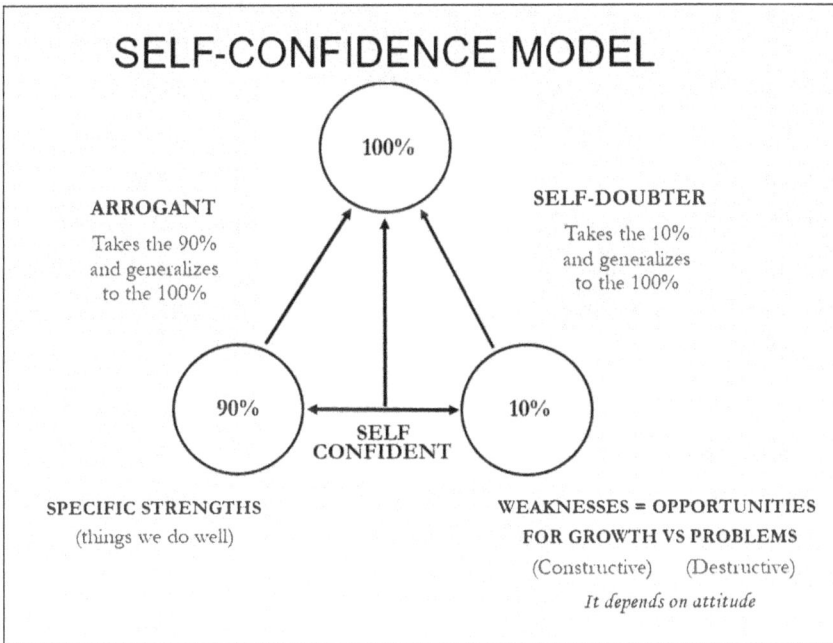

SELF-CONFIDENCE MODEL

100%

ARROGANT

Takes the 90% and generalizes to the 100%

SELF-DOUBTER

Takes the 10% and generalizes to the 100%

90% ← → 10%

SELF CONFIDENT

SPECIFIC STRENGTHS

(things we do well)

WEAKNESSES = OPPORTUNITIES

FOR GROWTH VS PROBLEMS

(Constructive)   (Destructive)

It depends on attitude

In the model highlighted in the above graph, self-confidence (SC) involves both Conscious Competence (CC) and Conscious Incompetence (CI). An Arrogant person is Consciously Competent (CC) and Unconsciously Incompetent (UI). In other words, they know what they do well but have no awareness of any weaknesses. They only learn from their strengths and only have half the learning potential of a SC individual who learns from what they well and also are aware of growth opportunities or weaknesses. The arrogant generalizes from the 90% to the 100% which operationalizes as "I do these things well that must mean I am great." The Self Doubter is Unconsciously Competent (UC) and Consciously Incompetent (CI) and generalizes from 10% weaknesses and has lost awareness of strengths. The Self Doubter has only half the learning potential of the SC person who learns from both their strengths and weaknesses. As discussed earlier this is in a minimum 5:1 ratio of CC (Strengths) to CI (weaknesses).

In the model above we are suggesting the minimum might be 5:1. (80%-20%) but ideally (90%-10%) in terms of strengths to weaknesses. There are 2 major reasons for the recommended 90-10 split. 1) It is human nature for individuals to focus on and relive negatives. For example, we go to a party with 20 people and forget the name of 1 person and then on the way home focus on "I can't believe I forgot John's name" and forget that we remembered 19. In sales, reps can make 9 out of 10 successful calls and get negative feedback on 1 call and feel totally rejected and evaluate the day as a nonsuccess. 2) We are often taught by our parents and significant others that we shouldn't talk positively about ourselves because that is bragging. We are not taught that reporting is OK but judging is not. Both the Self Doubter and Arrogant individuals are long-term issues for maintaining high levels of SC but for different reasons. The Arrogant person fails to be conscious of any weaknesses or growth opportunities and as a result can become incompetent as the external environment continues to evolve and require growth in terms of skills and knowledge to keep up. The self doubter is focused on weaknesses and can no longer consciously leverage their strengths to maximize their performance. The SC person views their weaknesses as growth opportunities rather than as problems. Being CC they have the confidence to approach weaknesses as opportunities and continue to both grow and consciously leverage their strengths

In the model Arrogant individuals are CC and UI. The arrogant person takes the CC and generalizes it to the 100% and doesn't know there are growth opportunities. "I am a good closer that must mean I am a great salesperson." They can be top performers on a short-term basis but don't grow long-term because they have no idea that there is room to grow. They are typically viewed negatively at an attitudinal level and are vulnerable to a coach attempting to point out growth opportunities. They view all feedback as negative and don't have the confidence to accept any feedback as positive. Coaches must continue to reinforce CC by asking arrogant individuals to self identify strengths before asking (not telling) about any areas of weakness. The best hockey coach I had was a master at helping us grow. Before practice, he would tap you on the shoulder and say he would like to see you after practice. We would work like crazy during practice expecting the worst, and he would begin with discussing all the things I was doing well for the first 14 minutes of a 15 minute meeting. At the end of the meeting, he would say by the way, can you stay with your check a little longer in the neutral zone. I thought Yes, that is a good idea, and I worked on the suggestion and became a better player. If he had started with the suggestion I probably couldn't wait to get out of the meeting. After the initial meetings, he had Weekly Development Meetings (WDMs), and we all looked forward to meeting as we became CC and better players. He changed the expectation from anticipating a problem to looking forward to a growth opportunity that would move a weakness into a strength and interact with our other strengths to improve our SC and subsequently our performance.

We always ask Sales reps about their meetings with coaches, do they have WDMs and what are their expectations for the meetings. The top performing reps with top coaches always look forward to their meetings as a growth opportunity rather than criticism or pointing out weaknesses. The top performers with less effective coaches expect the meetings to be focused on problems or negatives. There is no such thing as constructive criticism. Criticism is negative and creates Conscious Incompetence unless it follows a focus on creating CC then it is viewed as a growth opportunity rather than criticism.

The Self Doubter is UC and CI. In other words has forgotten and become de-sensitized to their strengths and focused on their weaknesses, In other words, they generalize from the 10% CI to the 100% "I don't do that so well that must mean I am no good."

Great coaches understand the difference between telling and asking. Self Confidence is CC. The best coaches ask individuals about their strengths and then their growth opportunities. This is not only effective for creating CC but also provides the opportunity to reinforce the strengths, potentially add to them and also understand what the sales rep is self-reinforcing. This also maximizes coaching time as the coach doesn't have to guess about the individual's CC and CI. Most coaches learn very quickly that you can't tell anyone anything, and it is difficult to impact positive change in attitudes and behaviors through compliance. Top coaches work from the inside out not the outside in.

A characteristic of top performers is they avoid the 'yes, but syndrome'. They learn to accept compliments with a simple Thank you. My favorite boxer was Muhammad Ali, and I always found his postfight interviews with Howard Cosell entertaining and humorous. Howard Cosell would compliment Muhammad and he would add to the compliment or mention another strength like "Float like a butterfly, sting like a bee."

When I first started doing presentations and facilitating workshops participants would come up and compliment me on the presentation and I would say "Yes but I didn't get through all the material." In the evaluation process, someone would rate me as average and indicate that I didn't complete the presentation. I negated the compliment and quickly learned to accept with a simple add-on like, "Thank you, I really enjoyed the group and appreciate your feedback." If I had time I might engage them further by asking, "What was your main takeaway?" or "what did you enjoy the most about the presentation."

"Have you experienced this in your work life?" This approach accomplishes two very important objectives. It reinforces the participant's feelings but is also a valuable learning experience for me. I am certain many readers have been in a sales presentation that is not quite connecting with the audience and needs a trigger to re-connect. Feedback from audiences about positive takeaways provides an excellent trigger.

Top performers and coaches not only learn to accept compliments but also how to give compliments vs flattery. The difference between a compliment and flattery is the difference between reporting and judging and relates back to our Self Confidence model. A report and compliment is specific and requires more energy and thought. Flattery is more judgmental and can be easily negated by the recipient. For example, "You are a great salesperson" vs. "I really enjoy your sales presentations. They flow nicely and display your ability to connect with a client." Relating to the self-confidence model, flattery generalizes from a specific strength to the 100% (i.e., great) whereas the compliment is very specific and requires more thought and energy. Also, notice the ideal compliment involves both the left side and right side of the brain, both factual and emotional. The recipient will immediately notice the difference as top performers typically receive flattery statements.

SC sales reps not only deal effectively with compliments they are also skilled at dealing with criticism and avoiding turning negative feedback into feelings of rejection. Call reluctance is turning negative feedback into lowering and internalizing feelings of low self worth and increasing levels of CI. As mentioned earlier, there is no such thing as constructive criticism unless it is clearly an attempt to provide a growth opportunity and genuinely attempting to help an individual. So how do we decide on the intent of an individual for giving us feedback? We can only observe behavior, but we often need to guess at intent. The first suggestion from most experts is to consider the source. This requires knowledge and experience with the source and a trusting relationship. Previous experience is the key to interpreting the intent of the source. For example, if the source is typically complimenting and highlighting strengths and then mentions something negative (ideally 5:1), it is more likely to be viewed as a growth opportunity and the source is more likely to be considered as attempting to be helpful. However, if the source is always pointing out negatives, it is unlikely that the recipient will view the feedback as helpful. The style of the source can be either a downside negative habit or an upside positive habit pattern. As a side note, it has been my experience that if a person is speaking negatively about others, they are probably talking negatively about you. It is a habit.

So how do we handle criticism and negative feedback to determine the intent of the source. If we trust the source: Strategy #1: Total acceptance "I will not do it anymore" and immediately change our behavior and follow their advice or suggestion based on trust of the source.If we don't trust the source: total apparent acceptance and continue the behavior. Do not waste any energy attempting to understand the intent of the source or implementing their advice. If we are uncertain we need to ask questions to determine the intent. "That behavior is a habit that is a trigger for me to trial close during my sales presentation, what would you recommend as a replacement for that trigger that would be more effective" If the source's intent is positive they will have a suggestion. If the intent is negative, there will be no recommendation for improvement but simply hollow criticism.

Self-Talk: An important component of developing Self Confidence. Learn to talk about yourself positively. At the beginning of our seminars, we ask participants to introduce themselves, and if we leave it as a simple open ended question, it is interesting how difficult it is for some participants. This will reflect the early conditioning from parents and the comfort in positive self talk. Another interesting strategy is to ask participants to introduce themselves by mentioning 5 strengths and 1 weakness. They often have difficulty talking about the 5 positives and generally broadcast the 1 negative. It is a test of the SC model and previous conditioning. It is important not to confuse Positive Mental Attitude (PMA) with CC. PMA is simply making generalized positive statements and is very fragile such as I am good or I am talented. CC is very specific such I have worked very hard at developing my sales tract for this specific product or client. PMA is like a balloon where one criticism can immediately deflate the balloon whereas SC is based on specific strengths (CC) and is robust and not easily deflated by external experiences and feedback. The general principle is promote the Self-Complimenter and Silence the Self-Criticizer.

Developing sales potential and maximizing performance requires mental practice and rehearsal. During my graduate studies, I had the opportunity to train elite Gymnasts in the importance of mental practice and rehearsal before their actual performance. Before the event, they had to successfully complete their routine mentally. As a result, during their routine they didn't have to think about completing their routine mentally which allowed them to be expressive with the judges. This is the same with sales presentations. To be aware of how the client is responding, it is essential that the sales rep has practiced the presentation and can be natural and expressive during the presentation and not worry about the successful completion of the presentation

When selling yourself in a job interview and promoting yourself in a company, Self Talk and a "Marketing Spiel" is the #1 tool we develop to train and counsel individuals on marketing and selling themselves during a job interview. The Marketing Spiel is in response to a sell question that inexperienced interviewers often ask. For example, "Tell me about yourself" This is an open ticket to mention everything in your background that highlights your experience that relates to the job opportunity.

The Spiel starts with your #1 strength, which is your reputation. Most successful teams and organizations and individuals have a reputation. Reputation is the first building block of SC. As a hockey coach, I always developed a reputation for my team and for each individual player. In my business, our company's reputation is: "We are the #1 company for predicting sales performance and retention." It is based on strengths and is not Hyperbole. We have over 30 million sales reps in our database, perform hundreds of predictive validation studies per year, and over four decades of experience. Our competitors claim the same but do not have the data or experience to substantiate the claim. As a result, it is easy to exploit their claims through a simple comparison of data to support their claims (i.e., not based on reality). On our team, we have the #1 prospector, the #1 relationship builder, and the #1 closer, etc.

Reputation is the number one strategy for coping with stress and performance slumps. The only way to shorten a slump is to get individuals and teams to focus and execute strengths (CC). The way to lengthen a slump is to get individuals and teams focused on weaknesses and create CI. Some sales coaches are always looking for weaknesses and what is wrong rather than strengths. It appears to be counter intuitive and based on their previous conditioning and experiences. I learned the hard way as a hockey coach and sales coach that the way to prolong a slump was to focus a practice or training session on correcting weaknesses. This approach simply reinforces and increases the awareness of incompetence (CI) and minimizes performance. I heard coaches say, "We are going to do this until we get it right." I learned from listening to top athletes and sales rep that the only way to get out of a slump was to go back to the proven basics and the foundation for their success and then continue to grow on the foundation. Coaching players when the team is winning is very easy. Everyone is excited and energized and it is the best time to run a demanding practice to improve conditioning and skills. When the team is losing the goal is get the team energized and feeling competent again. This can only be accomplished by working on strengths. The only way to maximize performance and increase the probability of winning or closing a sale is to execute on your strengths. You can't work on weaknesses during a game or during a sales presentation. It is so obvious that the only way to maximize performance is to only do what you do well as often as you can. The way to minimize your performance is to only do what you don't well as often as you can. Many coaches feel their main responsibility is to find and correct weaknesses rather than develop CC so sales reps can leverage their strengths without needing the coach.

Call Reluctance is often a major issue affecting sales performance and limiting the impact of Sales DNA and often learned through a gap between expectations and actual performance. A common fault of some sales organizations and coaches is setting performance expectations based on norms or averages. For example: In the first 3 months we expect 1 sale per week or 12 in the first quarter. OR our average sales process is 10-5-2-1 (10 calls, 5 discussions, 2 booked appointments, and 1 sale). As we will discuss in the next chapter, the only controllable is the 10 calls. So the rep during the first week averages 10-4-1-0. They might begin to think they are below average and can't sell, especially if they focus on the number of sales. In another example the rep averages 10-6-3-2. They might think they are great sales reps and possibly don't have to make the 10 calls, which is the only controllable. The only solution is to base expectations on their actual numbers and ensure that they continue to monitor their effectiveness based on controllables. If they call 10 prospects a day it is the role of the coach to turn activity into results and all experienced coaches are good at coaching the quality of effort and helping a sales rep with getting results from activity. Actual results based on uncontrollables can create many attitudinal issues and superstitious behaviors that are based exclusively on results. Attitudes such as Call Reluctance are based on recent experiences. It is often the reason top performers can become ineffective by focusing on results and becoming incompetent. In consulting with the NHL team, I had the privilege of meeting a top player at the end of his career who will be in the Hockey Hall of Fame. He was traded to another team and was expected to lead his new team and perform at the same levels as with his previous team. Of course, this was an unrealistic expectation, and the fans, coaches, and owners started to criticize him and he stopped doing the things that made him successful and started to focus on his weaknesses rather than strengths. The goal of the consulting process was simply to get him back to focusing on his strengths, executing his strengths, which resulted in performance increases that satisfied the fans who now had the opportunity to reinforce his performance.

Another attitudinal component of Sales DNA is being Self Directed or having an internal Locus of Control. Top performers score high on our Self Directed scale or internal locus of control. They believe they make it happen vs. being victims of circumstance or dependent on external factors. For example if you ask the reps to rate themselves on a scale from 5 agree to 1 definitely do not agree on the following item "Success is mostly luck" the Self Directed rep will typically answer 1 or 2, whereas the low locus of control rep will answer 4 or 5. Obviously some experiences created this attitude. The implications for coaching the low SD are significant. It is very difficult to get someone with a low SD to take responsibility for their performance if they believe their success is dependent on luck or external factors. They will blame many factors for their lack of success and will be involved with many "Ain't it awful sessions" with other nonachievers. They will be blaming the market, the products, the training, the brand, etc.

The problem is that it could be true or partially true. For example in recessionary markets, sales can be lower. Our research shows that during recessionary times the performance gap between high Sales DNA and low Sales DNA increases significantly. The high Sales DNA individuals continue to focus on the controllable components of performance, whereas the low Sales DNA become victims and give up on taking responsibility.

So how do we help coaches change attitudes. It is a technique called Cognitive Restructuring (CR). You can't tell an individual that they are wrong to have that negative habit of thought because there is probably an element of truth to their thoughts of being a victim of external environmental factors such as a recession. Through (CR) a coach explores the evidence and experiences the rep is basing the attitude on and attempts to ask about other evidence that they are not using that might get them thinking differently about the evidence they are using to formulate their attitude. Skilled professionals use empathy whereas someone not trained might use Sympathy. Empathy is understanding how and why they think a certain way and attempting to provide additional evidence to possibly modify or change their attitude. Sympathy is understanding and reinforcing their attitude to make them feel better as opposed to helping modify or change the attitude. Sympathy ends up enabling a person and maintaining the existing issue rather than modifying it.

CR is very different from PMA and an important differentiation for coaching and self talk. Many organizations will attempt to deal with attitudinal issues through motivational seminars and listening to motivational tapes and resources. They are great techniques for hyping up an individual's PMA but are typically short-term strategies with no permanent behavioral change unless the attitudinal change is based on additional information and a corresponding change in behavior. As a coach, I discovered that the impact of my pep talks lasted about as long as the national anthem.

Two final attitudes typical of top performers:

Commitment to their Career. They believe in their career and their company. They are proud to be in sales and are masters at networking and self promotion. They are the best source for other top potential sales candidates and view other top performers as valuable team members rather than competition.

Sense of Humor. An interesting debate is whether it is possible a train someone to have a Sense of Humor. High Sales DNA individuals often have a sense of humor because they are positive thinkers and they tend to see humor in many situations. As a result, they are fun to be around and tend to attract other positive thinkers.

In Summary, top performers are upside thinkers, focus on their strengths and are constantly looking for growth opportunities. They are SC and have full learning potential as they are CC and CI and learn from both their strengths and their weaknesses. Being CC gives the opportunity to view CI as a growth opportunity rather than a problem. Arrogant reps are also CC but are CI and lack awareness of growth opportunities and can become incompetent in times of change that require additional skills and knowledge. Both are aware of their strengths however the arrogant group is tougher to coach than the SC group as they are UI. To grow the arrogant group it is necessary to reinforce their CC before attempting to point out incompetence, as this approach will simply create conflict and potentially lower performance. The Self Confident group, the Self Doubters and the disengaged group are all CI. The self doubter and the disengaged are the opposite problem to coach because of the 'yes but syndrome'. Cognitive restructuring is a difficult process to coach as it takes a great deal of time and energy to slowly develop CC. It takes time and patience so it is best not to hire these attitudinal issues as most coaches don't have the patience or energy to make permanent attitudinal changes.

Because of the similarities and differences it can be confusing for recruiters to source and identify top performers with the high Sales DNA. For example in the de-selection screening process the focus is on negatives or what the candidate doesn't have and it could be any of the 3 groups who are CI. The Arrogant candidate is not CI and might be perceived as the best candidate. The paradigm shifts during the Selection process and is based on positives. The decision to hire a candidate is an investment decision. All new candidates require investments and a valid prediction of the potential return on the investment. Ideally internal recruiters and hiring managers are well matched to the characteristics of a top performer and can understand and evaluate candidates based on their fit to the career and opportunity. Based on the SC model, both the Self Confident and Arrogant candidates might be viewed negatively by a recruiter who is uncomfortable with Consciously Competent individuals and views both as arrogant. The self doubter might be viewed as more likeable. Super Sales Recruiters possess high Sales DNA, ideally in the 17% and well-matched (empathetic) to the sales professionals they are attempting to recruit.

WILL DO HABITS include both attitudes and behaviors. Attitudes are typically associated with Quality and Effort with the quantity aspects of sales performance. Permanent change and top performance requires a change in both attitude and behavior. If there is only a change in attitude with no change in behavior the behavior will erode the attitude; a change in behavior with no change in attitude the attitude will eventually erode the behavior

Let's now look at Habits of Behavior.

> The first step of retention is building in basic survival habits that will give coaches the opportunity to "coach" rather than "coax."

CHAPTER 5

Habits of Behavior – The "WILL DO"

A consistent finding of research is that most top organizations and coaches know how to train the sales process, sales skills and provide the expertise to continually grow "trainable" talent. However, the major reason sales candidates don't survive or perform well is the new sales candidate doesn't initiate the sales process through prospecting or business development activity to utilize all the training and skill development. In other words, they "CAN" do the job but don't make the necessary daily commitments to create basic habits to ensure they survive. In all sales organizations when we ask what differentiates the successful from the unsuccessful it is always an effort or work habit issue. A unique aspect of our approach to training and coaching is helping new candidates develop basic survival habits. We often ask coaches and leaders, "Is it possible to work hard every day and fail as a sales representative in your company"? The answer is "yes but it would be difficult."

One of my most interesting consulting experiences was with a large financial services organization that had a two month extensive head office training program for new recruits. The program was amazing and included product knowledge, sales process, role-plays, development of scripts etc. We asked the sales leaders why reps were failing with such an extensive training program. The answer was "they don't see enough potential clients to utilize the training." We asked how much time in the training program do you dedicate to developing prospecting or business development activities. The answer was we "don't have time in the training program." The problem was further exacerbated by requiring all new representatives who were not performing up to the standard at three months to attend an additional one month head office special training program to help solve the performance problem. Again, the focus of the program was on the development of skills and sales process. You can guess the impact of the additional training, as the focus was on HOW to do the job and not addressing the real issue of "WILL" they do the job. The corporate culture was unconsciously reinforcing individuals for not working hard and creating a "nonperformance corporate culture" often at the expense of the individuals who were working hard and performing. It is a waste of resources and money training a "WILL" issue" with a "CAN" approach.

When you train a lazy, low activity sales representative,

You get a lazy, low activity skilled sales representative.

The first step of retention is building in basic survival habits that will give coaches the opportunity to "coach" rather than "coax." The role of coaches is to turn effort into results and most are extremely skilled at coaching. However, dealing with attitudinal or effort issues is much more difficult as coaches are now required to track or replace habit patterns that are ingrained through years of reinforcement and experience. Coaxing is attempting to motivate individuals to work hard and develop new successful habits.

During our workshops on developing Self-Managers we ask the participants to rate themselves on a 5 point scale from

5=excellent to 1= poor for the Talent and Habits components of the Performance equation and then rate the best salesperson they know and then compare them to their self-assessments. The biggest gap is always on the WILL DO or habits components and focused on the Effort factor. It is interesting as we have previously discussed and arrived at agreement that Attitude and Effort are 100% in their control. The question is WHY and why they don't simply agree to work harder. As mentioned previously the common characteristic of all top performers is they work hard and have a strong work ethic. It is a habit that is ingrained though early life experiences and continues throughout their entire life in both their personal and professional lives. It becomes part of their DNA. They probably had a paper route, lemonade stand, part time business cutting lawns or shovelling snow, or part time jobs while studying. Second incomes on the weekend.

It is called self-commitment and is an internal process that is a key differentiator from commitments that are an external process.

Self-commitment never stops but is always present and is often confused by recruiters and coaches. For example, being the President of a club or Association is a commitment that doesn't necessarily reflect self-commitment. Being the President requires an individual to follow a set of procedures and structure that have been passed on from President to President. It is not self-initiated effort but rather structure initiated effort. Often, self-commitment shows itself in part as self-initiated efforts towards personal and professional development. It is easy to spot in a resume or in an interview. Constant upgrading and development of trainable talent will be obvious in certificates, courses, participation in workshops and seminars, associations, reading materials etc. community and volunteer work,

The Self-Commitment Race Track

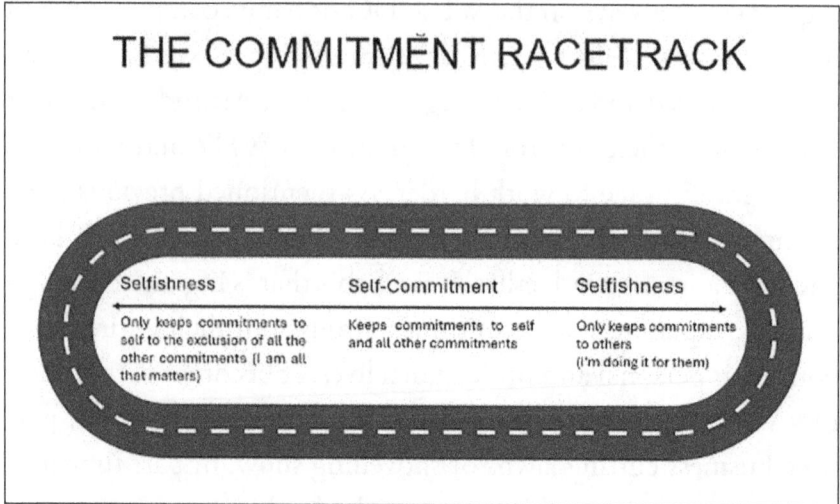

THE COMMITMENT RACETRACK

Selfishness	Self-Commitment	Selfishness
Only keeps commitments to self to the exclusion of all the other commitments (I am all that matters)	Keeps commitments to self and all other commitments	Only keeps commitments to others (I'm doing it for them)

The reason we call it a race track rather than a continuum is that it is often confusing to determine the difference between a self-commitment and external commitments that might be interpreted as either selfish or selfless. Self-commitment is keeping commitments to both yourself and to others. Selfish is keeping commitments to yourself at the expense of keeping commitments to others. For example, you commit to helping an associate with their sales process and you fail to show up at the meeting because you decided to work out instead in your home gym. Selfless is keeping commitments to others and not to yourself. On your way home you plan on going to the gym to work out and your manager calls you and says you are needed back at the office immediately, so you turn around and head back to the office and cancel your workout. The bottom line is if we don't look after ourselves we might not have the energy or health to look after our other commitments. The reason we lack or lose self-commitment is because it is easier and more superficially rewarding to respond to external factors rather than to internal self-imposed demands. Others will pat us on the back for doing what they want us to do which is far more rewarding if we never learn to pat ourselves on the back. A key attribute of self-managers is the ability to self-reinforce for keeping commitments. Think of early our conditioning from parents, teachers, coaches, and managers:

"Do it for me"
"If you do this I will give you"
"One for the Gipper"
"My job is on the line"

We become externally controlled and others know how get us to do what they want us to do. In some situations, it is confusing whether we are selfish or selfless. For example, we are coaching our kids team and we are really enjoying it. Is it looking after ourselves or keeping a commitment to our family? At times, it doesn't matter as we can accomplish both commitments without interfering with other commitments such as our career. In most situations we can usually keep both commitments. For example, to your manager "I can't come immediately but I can be there for you in a few hours and be able to work with you until we complete the job." Is playing golf with a client who is also a friend, a self-commitment or a commitment to our career?

Keeping self-commitments over external commitments is further complicated by an interesting aspect of human nature. The closer someone is to us the more we take them for granted and as a result are more committed to them. The old story of the plumber who fixes his neighbors plumbing before his own. We are closest to ourselves and then to our family and then to our friends and associates. The consequence is we take ourselves for granted and often have the least commitment to ourselves.

As highlighted in a future chapter on Managing Energy and lifestyle planning it will be evident that looking after ourselves is important but is often the most overlooked commitment. It is heartbreaking in my consulting with top performers who are very successful but forgot to bring their health or their family along for the ride. Keeping self-commitments is an essential ingredient of self-management and an essential ingredient of true success. Ideally it becomes part of our DNA and we learn how to reinforce our self-commitments and live a long healthy successful life.

A key characteristic of sales performers is they are trusted by their clients and trustworthy. In psychology we are trained that the easiest way to start a trusted interpersonal relationship is to search for communality. The technique is simply to ask questions to explore common interests such as movies, theatre, books, travel, hobbies, etc. Once you discover a common interest it can open an engaging conversation that will lead to other common interests or activities. In sales, it is always recommended to do a little research on the individual and or company you are meeting with prior to your first meeting. Online social media sites provide a lot of potential material to start the communality discussion. Stage 2 of trust in a sales presentation is competence. The sales presentation serves the purpose of a fact find to discover any needs as well as demonstrate competence. The final stage and highest level of trust is commitment. It is essential to keep and follow up on commitments established during the sales meeting. Missing any commitment will immediately create a trust problem that will be impossible to repair. We have all experienced the situation where a friend or associate failed to keep a commitment for a meeting or party or attending a social event. If this occurs on a regular basis it is difficult to trust that they will keep any future commitments.

We often hear politicians making promises during election campaigns which we interpret as commitments they will keep if they are elected. If the promises are not kept we realize that they were not commitments and we not only lose trust but also begin to question their competence. Later we will discuss the SEVERE problem of coaching sales reps that don't keep their commitments to daily activities.

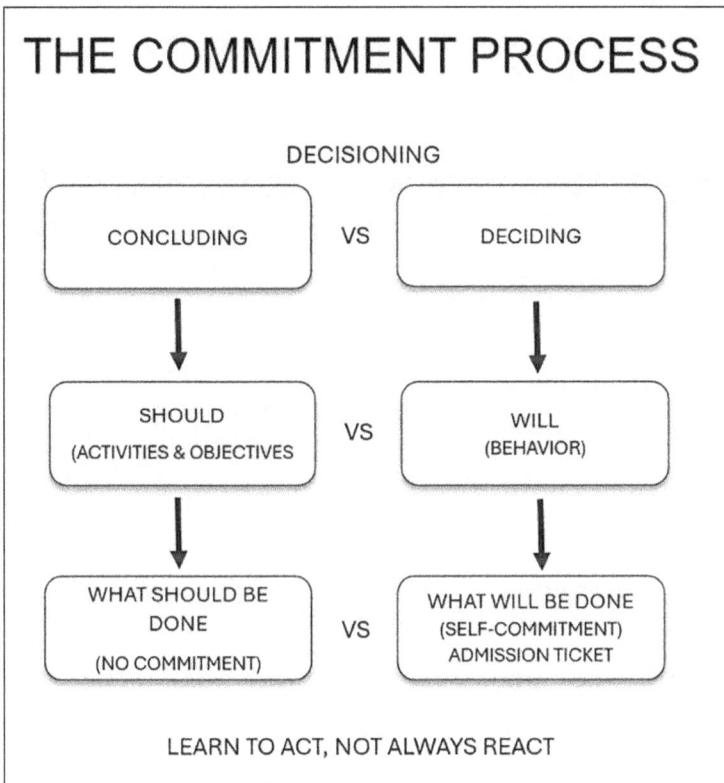

THE COMMITMENT PROCESS

DECISIONING

| CONCLUDING | VS | DECIDING |

SHOULD
(ACTIVITIES & OBJECTIVES

VS

WILL
(BEHAVIOR)

WHAT SHOULD BE DONE
(NO COMMITMENT)

VS

WHAT WILL BE DONE
(SELF-COMMITMENT)
ADMISSION TICKET

LEARN TO ACT, NOT ALWAYS REACT

As evidenced in the above graph, the commitment process requires decisions as opposed to conclusions. A decision is what will be done whereas a conclusion is what should be done.

The biggest issue with effective psychological time management is confusing conclusions with decisions. We often make numerous conclusions to arrive at one decision. Conclusions are a major waste of time and energy.

The start of the process is usually a suggestion from an external source that we should do something. For example, our kids or spouse might recommend that "you should exercise and lose weight." So, we start to think that we should begin to exercise but we are busy today so maybe tomorrow. Tomorrow, we get busy at work and make a plan to start tomorrow. The should process continues until we make a decision (ie a commitment) and perhaps jog for 30 mins at lunch. As we mature and evaluate some of the conclusions we made earlier in our lives that never became decisions the should haves become could haves. We have season hockey tickets and one friend I take to one game every year always says ' I could have made the NHL if I wasn't so busy at school rather developing my skills."

The biggest should in sales revolves around prospecting and business development as it is the most challenging and important activity. If we have a coach who tells us what we should do or how many calls we should make. It naturally leads to a conclusion rather than a decision. Shoulds are compliance rather than a decision and a commitment. With a conclusion the day starts with I should make my calls but I want to talk to John about the game last night. While I am talking to John I am thinking that I should be making my calls. After meeting with John, I will get my coffee to provide the caffeine hit to get me ready to make my calls. If it remains a should it is easy to find other things to interfere with making a decision to make the calls. At the end of the day, we drive home and feel guilty that we didn't make the calls and we should double the number of calls the next day to compensate. If we had made the decision and kept the commitment to make the calls, our drive home would be very different. We would be able to self-reinforce for making the calls and feeling like we had a successful day. Keeping our commitments allow us to be successful every day and it is totally within our control. Dealing with shoulds is a waste of energy and psychologically exhausting and are guilt producers.

Dealing with career situations also requires effective decision making and relates to being responsible and accountable.

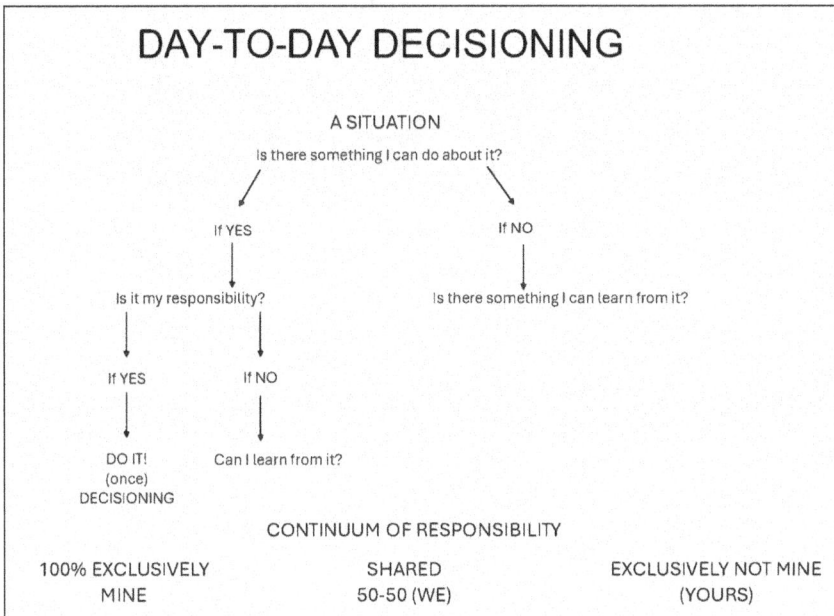

DAY-TO-DAY DECISIONING

A SITUATION

Is there something I can do about it?

If YES   If NO

Is it my responsibility?   Is there something I can learn from it?

If YES   If NO

DO IT!   Can I learn from it?
(once)
DECISIONING

CONTINUUM OF RESPONSIBILITY

100% EXCLUSIVELY MINE	SHARED 50-50 (WE)	EXCLUSIVELY NOT MINE (YOURS)

In any situation, "Is there anything I can do about it?" is the first question that begins the decisioning process. If the answer is No, the second question "is there something I can learn from it." If No, no additional energy is necessary to make a decision and there no lingering should that requires future energy. If the answer is YES, then the second question is "Is it my responsibility?" If the answer is NO then no decision is required. This is extremely important for coaches and parents. If it is not your responsibility and you make it your responsibility then you are inadvertently teaching someone NOT to be responsible and that you will deal with any of their situations. As a result, a parent or coach will take responsibility for solving a problem rather than teaching someone how to solve the problem or deal with the situation. If it is 100% your responsibility, then the decision is made for you.

Just DO IT and don't waste energy thinking if you should do it. If it is a shared responsibility, it becomes that excellent training and coaching opportunity where the coach can discuss who is responsibility for which elements of the situation or problem. The coach can demonstrate that they are being responsible and accountable and set the expectation of accountability for the other individual(s) who share the responsibility.

Managing Effort and Goal Setting

A common question asked by coaches during our workshops is how we avoid compliance when we need to set goals and objectives for our sales team. There are 3 potential goal-setting strategies:

1. MBO (Management By Objectives)
2. MBE (Management By Effort)
3. MBR (Management by Results)

To gain commitment to activities, we could start the performance management process with objectives or goals by simply asking a sales rep how much money they would like to make this year. Or are you planning any trips or major purchases this year that will require extra income. Goals are what we want but without a plan on how to make the extra money, goals are simply dreams or wants. If we start with objectives, everybody wants to make a lot of money and be successful. The question is always the price they are willing to pay to achieve their goal or objectives. The same is true if we start with Results and MBR. The problem with both MBO and MBR is we are going the wrong way on a one way street which can end up MBC (Management By Crisis) if the results or objectives are not achieved. We then look for reasons 'Why 'and the answer could be a talent issue that requires skills training or additional product knowledge. It could be an effort problem. It could be market conditions or any number of external factors. The major problem is we don't know if it is a "CAN DO" or "WILL DO" issue that will define the solution.

In both MBO and MBR, the process starts with a desire not a commitment. If the coach then explores the plan to achieve the goals and results, the plan becomes a should not necessarily a commitment. If the coach develops the activity plan or if the coach sets the goals, there is only compliance and little commitment.

Effort is the only way to move from objectives to results. Start with effort and commitment and move to results and objectives. It is obvious that individuals will have a greater degree of commitment to decisions they have been involved in making. Also the greater the control over the decisions and objectives the greater the potential for commitment. If an individual has 100% control and 100% responsibility over a decision there is no reason not to keep the commitment. The coach will never need to ask why unless it is a one-time occurrence. In other words, if the individual has a history of keeping commitments and not keeping a commitment is an unusual occurrence then there might be an external or noncareer related situation that interfered with keeping the commitment. However, if this is a recurring problem, the coach has a much more serious issue and a trust problem. BUT, most importantly has identified the issue as a WILL problem and doesn't need to waste energy treating it as a CAN issue.

The simple solution to effective goal setting is to start with commitment. Establish what price (commitment) the individual is willing to pay. The focus is on effort, the 100% controllable and then move forward to results which are not 100% controllable. This avoids the issue of WHERE the results are coming from vs HOW to maximize performance and results. This also avoids the sophomore jinx in sales planning and reduces anxiety about uncontrollable factors. A classic example is the lottery sale that inflates results. For example, the sales rep landed a few very large contracts or what is often referred to in the sales jargon as whales. The rep and the coach both worry about where to find more whales as opposed to how to find more whales.

Action absorbs anxiety. Focusing on action and activity which are controllable reduces anxiety and wasting energy to cope with the stress associated with the anxiety. The energy can be focused on performance and the rep can be successful every day and rewarded for keeping daily commitments. Not worrying about WHERE and possibly WHEN or if there will ever be another whale but rather increasing the probability of finding another whale. Also, the daily activity will maximize performance and results. There will be sales and successes to help the rep keep score. The key is to start with activity and evaluate how close we are moving toward the objectives. Over time we begin to establish the results from our commitment levels and can make a decision on whether or not to increase the level of commitment or price we are willing to pay OR focus on quality.

The simple solution to avoiding the Sophomore jinx and avoiding the confusion of identifying HOW vs WILL issues is demonstrated in the table presented below outlining a simple sales process. This example is simplistic and presented to demonstrate the value and advantages of the MBE goal setting strategy.

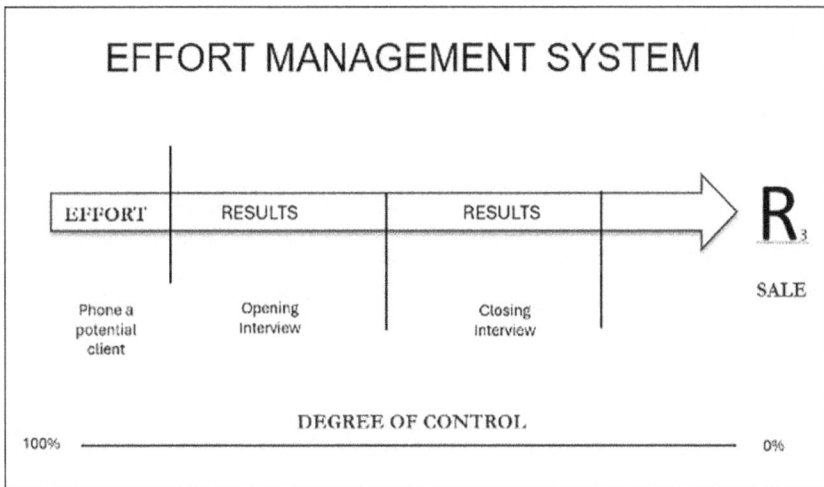

EFFORT MANAGEMENT SYSTEM

EFFORT	RESULTS	RESULTS	R_3
Phone a potential client	Opening Interview	Closing Interview	SALE

DEGREE OF CONTROL

100% ————————————————————— 0%

Degree of Control

As evidenced in the above graph, start with a commitment to effort that is 100% Controllable. This defines the Quantity of the initial commitment. In a simple sales example, it could be phoning or visiting a client or prospect. The first result (R1) is keeping the commitment and completing the sales presentation or fact finding interview to the best of the current ability level. This allows the individual to self-reinforce for keeping the commitment and doing their best. This also allows the coach to reinforce the result and more importantly provides a coaching opportunity. The coach can ask; "what worked well?" (conscious competence), "What did you learn or would you do differently?" (growth opportunity), "What are the next steps?" (Coaching opportunity - maybe presentation skills, trial closing or closing skills, etc). The coaching opportunity will help the coach improve the quality of the commitment and increase the probability of closing for the second or closing interview. As we move from the opening interview to the closing interview there less control as the client controls the agreement to a closing interview but the better the quality of the opening interview the greater the probability for the second interview and R2. If the rep is able to close and book the second, closing interview the same process occurs as outlined in R1. The rep and coach both get to reinforce the result and continue to improve the skills and quality of the effort. The coach also gets another coaching opportunity to help develop the rep to close for the sale. The third result R3 is closing the sale. A sale gives the coach the opportunity to reinforce the rep for both the activity and results. Obviously a very positive experience for both the rep and the coach. As outlined, the degree of control starts at 100 and ends with 0% as the client controls the buying decision. In our workshops, we always ask the top rep if they can guarantee a sale today. The answer is always no. This answer always surprises the new and inexperienced reps. The next question is "Can you guarantee talking to a potential client today?" and the answer is usually yes but not always. Experienced, successful reps have sufficient skills and experience to have more influence the deeper they go into the sales process but can only be in total control of their activity. Monitoring and reinforcing performance and success over controllables reduces the changes for call reluctance and the reduction of self-confidence by promoting conscious competence rather than conscious incompetence.

Let's define effort and outline and summarize the relationship and importance of attitude and effort in predicting sales performance, success and results. In a sales context effort is planned activities that are controllable and directly related to performance. NOT planned activities that are controllable and not related to performance. That is busy work. Busy work is the most common strategy for nonperformers to justify their lack of quality activity commitments and rationalize their nonperformance. Many can work long hours and it is easy for a coach to misinterpret busy work as quality effort.

It takes a high Sales DNA individual to have the ability to take on the energy and commitment necessary to be proactive and initiate the start of the sales process on a consistent, daily basis.

Effort is the quantity of effort and attitude impacts but is not necessarily exclusively the determinant of the quality of effort as talent also reflects quality. Quality effort is the foundation of sales performance. A sales rep who takes control of both effort and attitude will perform up to their current potential and be considered successful. Because we never perform up to ultimate potential and we continue to increase our potential throughout our career there is always the potential for the 'yes, but' syndrome. For example, "yes but I can do better" is always a true statement. High Sales DNA reps will constantly strive for perfection but never achieve it. Success is reaching our current potential by taking control of both attitude and effort. It is obvious, if we perform up to our potential we are successful and will maximize our results. WILL issues are increases in performance that require either additional effort or more effective, quality effort. More effective effort could be attitudinal and/or a training requirement, however, effort will always be the solution for increasing performance.

If a rep is working hard and controlling the front end of the sales process not only will the rep be able to identify where they are comfortable and need training but the coach will also be able to easily identify training issues through role-plays and joint field work. Attitudinal issues are easy to identify if the effort is consistent and quantifiable. Identifying CAN and WILL issues begin to identify and define the role of a coach. Coaching is facilitating the execution of effort and consulting on the quality of effort and helping to turn effort into performance. Coaxing is attempting to get reps to work hard over which a coach has zero control and is a waste of energy. It is the main reason coaches burnout. Attempting to take control and responsibility over things they don't control, It also creates dependency and interferes with the rep feeling responsible as the rep learns that if they don't take responsibility for their effort and behavior the coach will.

The fundamental foundation of developing and coaching self-managers is our Admission Ticket (AT) concept. The AT is not only the key to the survival and growth of a new sales rep. it also is the foundation for coaching reps and building a performance based sales team. It defines the performance standards for remaining on a sales team and sets the value a coach places on their time and expertise. Finally, it is the key to a long term, healthy career and life. We will start the AT discussion with how the application of the concept will ensure the survival and success of a new sales candidate.

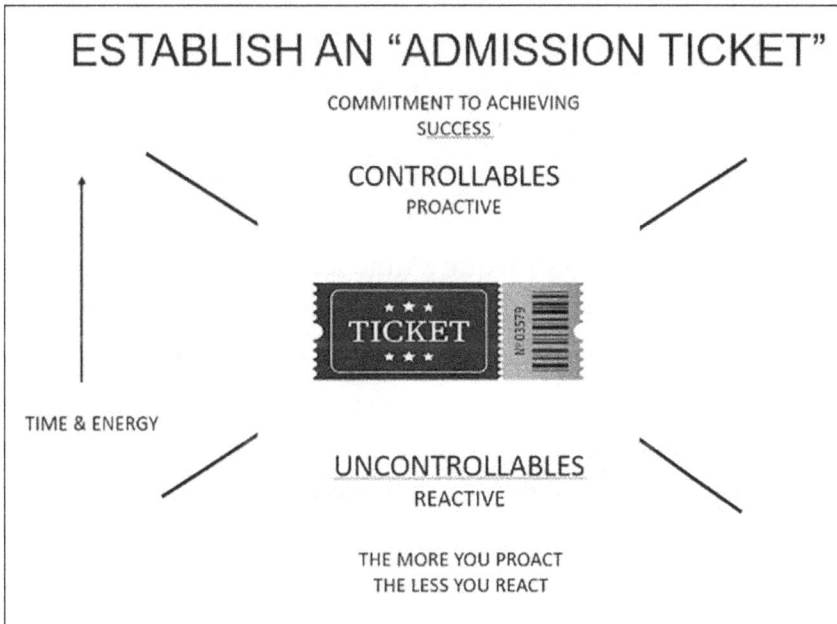

ESTABLISH AN "ADMISSION TICKET"

COMMITMENT TO ACHIEVING
SUCCESS

CONTROLLABLES
PROACTIVE

TICKET

TIME & ENERGY

UNCONTROLLABLES
REACTIVE

THE MORE YOU PROACT
THE LESS YOU REACT

In any given day in a busy sales environment there are any number of activities and actions that potentially require the allocation of time and energy. As evidenced in the diagram, the AT is the foundation and the essential ingredient for a successful sales career. Above the AT foundation we have the proactive, controllable activities that form our effort profile which is the key to understanding the awareness of the commitments necessary to survive and excel in a sales career. Below the AT, are the reactive uncontrollable things that vary from day to day but require allocation of our energies and can interfere with keeping the AT and other controllable commitments. The reactive, uncontrollable can be both work and lifestyle related. For example, a potential client might call with a service request or want more information about pricing or product. There might be a fire drill that requires everyone to leave the building. A sales leader or executive drops into the office and calls a quick meeting to discuss a new market development. A major client calls to re-schedule a morning meeting to the afternoon. The power goes out and all the computers go down and you lose part of a presentation you have been working on. A surprise birthday lunch for one of your key service team that requires your attendance. Other external lifestyle factors can also require time and energy. A flat tire on the way to work. A call to the school that your child is not feeling well and needs to be picked up. A call from home about a household problem that requires your time or expertise. We know the list of possibilities and have experienced many aspects that can require and drain our time and energy. The danger is that the reactive uncontrollables could take all our time or energy and we don't keep our foundation AT commitment and have nothing to reinforce and evaluate as being accomplished for the day. The solution is how we establish the AT.

The secret to surviving in a sales career is simple and has 100% agreement of all successful sales reps and leaders. Develop a daily prospecting habit. As one sales manager put it" the best way to improve sales is to talk to more people who might want to buy your product."

As mentioned previously, we always ask sales leaders and reps " is it possible to work hard every day and fail" The answer is yes but it would be difficult if not impossible. We then ask how much time and energy do you allocate in your initial training to developing a prospecting habit. Again, the answer is we don't have time as we need to train product and sales process. We then ask how many of your reps fail because they don't know the product or are not trained in the sales process. The answer is usually zero. It is mind boggling they identify the problem but continue to avoid the simple solution. Establishing the AT is almost the guarantee of at least survival.

The essential characteristics of the admission ticket:

100% controllable

Objective and measurable If the AT is not objective and measurable it can be easily avoided or the data can be misleading. For example, we have seen reps indicate that their AT is making calls every day rather than making 10 calls every day.

MOST IMPORTANT. It is the rock bottom daily commitment. In other words, no matter what happens at an uncontrollable, reactive level, the individual has sufficient time and energy to fulfil the AT commitment. The AT is impossible to rationalize for noncompletion due to external factors. This is the key to survival. Build the AT as the #1 career priority for any available time or energy.

Benefits of AT

The AT can be either a guilt producer or a guilt reducer. When we pay the daily price, there is no guilt on the way home as we accomplished our #1 priority commitment and looked after our career. Once we develop a habit, if we break the habit we feel guilty and the guilt provides an uncomfortable feeling and negative consequence of not looking after our career. From reinforcement theory we know that a negative consequence will extinguish the behavior and reduce the probability of not completing the AT again.

The AT saves time and energy as it is the #1 priority and is never a should but rather a decision that doesn't require any additional energy. It also helps prevent burnout by providing some positive return on energy. There is never a day of exclusively putting out fires with nothing being accomplished.

There is always an opportunity to self-evaluate a day as having some level of success. Sometimes on very busy days that have been filled with reactive uncontrollables, keeping the AT is an extremely powerful opportunity to self-reinforce. We can pat ourselves on the back for keeping our AT on a day that was extremely challenging because of all the interference.

It is the 1 habit that ensures survival and once survival is assured, provides the opportunity to focus on success. A major contributor to personal power is feeling in control of your career and success.

Once the AT has been established and becomes an habitual habit like brushing your teeth, it is a very simple planning and coaching process to increase performance and sales results. For example if a rep has an AT of 10 calls a day, after a specific period of time, we will know the quality of the activity and the results from both the quantity and quality of the activity. Let's look at a three-month window and we know that 10 calls per day has resulted in 5 opening interviews and 2 closing interviews and 1 sale worth $100 in commissions. There were 20 workdays per month and 60 days in the three-month window that resulted in 60 sales and $6,000 in commissions. In the planning session the rep wants to increase the commissions by 100% to $12,000 over the next three-months.

There are only 4 ways to improve performance and results:

Work more consistently. This would only be relevant is the rep missed some days but for simplicity let's assume it was a habitual habit

Work harder. We could simply double the AT to 20 calls a day.

Work smarter or improve the quality of the activity through training and coaching and increase the number of sales to 2 a day

Work Harder and Smarter. Continue improving the ratios through training and coaching and increasing the AT.

In Summary. Hard work (an effort habit) is a characteristic of all successful sales reps and leaders, It is typically a habit or work ethic that is developed early and continues throughout an individual's life. It becomes habitual and an integral part of our Sales DNA. It is the reason past effort always predicts future effort. If someone is lazy in the past they will be lazy in the future. Trainers and coaches love high effort sales reps as they receive an immediate performance increase from their efforts and expertise. The foundation of the effort habit is self-commitment. It comes from inside the individual (ie self-management) and develops and grows through self-reinforcement. The habit becomes habitual and does not require additional daily energy to make a decision to keep commitments. The decision has been made so all the energy is invested in accomplishing the commitments rather than spending energy making the decision. It should now be obvious the reason only 17% of the population has Sales DNA and the potential to be a top sales performer. The next chapter will explore how to create habitual habits when many external reinforcers tend to take us away from self-commitments and self-reinforcement and create dependency on outside factors.

" No matter how successful, or after the best day, best week, best month, best quarter, or best year, successful sales people never stop "loading the front end." "

CHAPTER 6

Building Habits – Making Habits Habitual

I once asked a room full of sales managers: "What's the one habit that guarantees a new rep will survive their first year?" Without hesitation, they all said the same thing: "Consistent prospecting." Then I asked: "So why do 60% of your new hires fail in year one?" Long silence. They all knew the answer, their reps weren't making prospecting a habit. Knowing what to do and actually doing it consistently are two entirely different things.

The starting point to creating a new habit is self-commitment and making a decision (will do) rather than a conclusion (should do). As soon as we decide that we will do something, we have a habit. The next step is to make it habitual like brushing our teeth or wearing a seat belt. We don't need to think about doing it, we just do it. It becomes automatic. There is no wasted energy deciding whether to do it, and if we don't do it, which rarely happens, we feel guilty.

Habits begin with self-commitment and then, by our late teens or early twenties, through reinforcement and motivation they become habitual and part of our DNA. There is a debate in the psychological literature about how long it takes to make a habit habitual.

Some trainers cite 21 days, others say 66 days, and neuroscientists suggest it varies by complexity. Our research shows it's not about time, it's about reinforcement density. A rep who makes 10 calls daily with immediate self-reinforcement can make it habitual in two weeks. A rep who makes 10 calls sporadically, waiting for external validation from prospects or managers, may never make it habitual.

To refine the theory from our perspective, it requires one second to make a decision and develop a habit, but it requires internal self-reinforcement and motivation to make it habitual. The number of times or days to make it habitual depends on the strength and effectiveness of the reinforcement.

Throughout our lives we continually develop new habits, both good and bad. To begin a sales career or continue to grow in any chosen career path, it is essential to examine our existing habits and understand how they became habitual. In almost all cases, they were initially developed through external reinforcement or influences, such as parents, peers, and teachers, and became automatic and self-reinforcing. The habits could be both attitudinal or behavioral, and the external reinforcers begin early in our lives. For example, did parents and teachers reinforce us for talking positively about ourselves or were we taught that was bragging? Did we learn to earn our allowance or was it given to us? At school, did teachers spend more time and energy on students who were working hard and achieving or on underachieving, behavioral problem students? Are our athletic and sports programs set up to reinforce performance and achievement or participation and mediocrity? Our learned habits impact our future career success, especially in a sales career that is performance based and requires the efficient and effective allocation of our energies when we only totally control our performance and have little control over the results of our efforts. As discussed earlier, results such as the buying decision are controlled by others and only influenced by the sales performer.

In all careers, our success is not only determined by our on-the-job habits but also our lifestyle habits. We will discuss managing success and lifestyle factors in chapter 9, as a long-term successful career in sales requires energy. Having the energy to invest in a sales career also requires investments in self and family.

As highlighted, habits start from the outside or external reinforcers and then, if motivational, move to the inside and become internal and self-reinforcing. As a result, bad habits are very difficult to break as we have become dependent on the external starting point and the internal self-reinforcement. We need to eliminate both the internal and external reinforcers to break a habit. The solution to creating a new habit appears very simple and straightforward. Start from the inside (self-commitment) and self-reinforce for keeping the commitment. As a result, we can be successful every day and not be dependent on outside, uncontrollable factors but rather be self-reliant and 100% in control of our feelings of competence and self-worth. Any external factors that complement and reinforce our commitments will be the icing on the cake rather than the cake itself.

The Admission Ticket: Building the Survival Habit

Step one in a sales career is to survive. As mentioned previously, when we ask sales leaders and representatives what daily habit would guarantee the survival of a new representative. In all cases, it is prospecting or daily business development activities. As one VP of Sales said, "Talking to more prospects who might want to buy your product or service." The next question concerns quantity. How many calls or contacts would guarantee success? There is no single answer, but all agree that making and keeping a commitment to a controllable, measurable activity defined as an "Admission Ticket" is the starting point and the major reason for the failure to survive of new representatives. Once a daily Admission Ticket is habitual, the role of a coach in improving performance and results is simplified. The coach now knows it is not a "will issue." The role of the coach might be to increase the quantity or the quality of the activity. However, without consistent effort, the coach might inadvertently treat a "WILL Issue" with a "CAN" approach. In other words, train an individual who is not working hard how to not work hard better. In reinforcement terms, this actually reinforces an individual for not working hard. With consistent effort, the coach has a lot to coach, as the representative has several prospect experiences to discuss with the coach. We will explore this further in a later chapter. Our consulting experiences demonstrate that most coaches are very well trained to coach and are effective at helping turn effort into performance. Very few are trained or have the patience to coax and get representatives with a poor work ethic to work hard.

Once the survival habit is in place, coaching options include working harder, working smarter, or working harder and smarter. Top performers are fun and challenging to coach and tremendous ambassadors to the sales team and corporation. Top sales performers who survive then develop different types of on-the-job success habits. To mention just a few:

They always ask for referrals from clients after they earn the right through good service and an established client relationship. Our top rep takes clients out to lunch every six months to maintain relationships and reinforce referrals. He gets lots of referrals.

They prepare and mentally rehearse before every key client interview and sales presentation.

They are respectful of the time of others and always on time for meetings and interviews.

They close after identifying a need of a client out of respect for the client to reduce anxiety.

They seek out advice from other top performers and resources to improve. They schedule weekly development meetings with their coaches and managers.

They compliment others, such as the service team, for helping them, often with lunches or small gifts like a Starbucks gift card.

They often mentor new, hard-working representatives.

If asked, they willingly share ideas and experiences at team and corporate meetings. They know the better the corporate brand and reputation, the better for them.

They promote the company and its products and help recruit other top performers.

They avoid bad situations like "ain't it awful" sessions, gossiping with negative complainers or lazy representatives, and two-martini lunches.

Most Important: No matter how successful, or after the best day, best week, best month, best quarter, or best year, they never stop "loading the front end." Their survival habit remains the foundation of their continued success. They don't know where the results will come from, but they know how to get results, and they know their current Admission Ticket will create the same results. To get more results, they can work harder, smarter, or harder and smarter. This is the antidote to the sophomore jinx. It's not about where results come from, but how they are achieved.

Understanding Reinforcement Theory

This brings us to the most powerful principle of psychology and human behavior: Reinforcement Theory. It works on every species, from humans to goldfish. There are two types of reinforcers, internal and external. External reinforcers come from all our life experiences as outlined previously. Internal reinforcers are the only truly motivational factors that maintain long-term habits. External reinforcers only become motivational if they are internalized.

Many individuals confuse reinforcement and motivation. Basically, you can't motivate anyone unless you provide reinforcement that is valued and internalized. As a hockey coach, the impact of my pep talk before a game lasted about as long as the national anthem. If the players were not ready or motivated to play, anything I would say would have little or no impact. Top sales performers are motivated by a mix of money, challenge, people, service, and recognition. Money is a major factor, but once they become successful and are making a lot of money, they continue to work hard because money is simply a way of keeping score and the other internal factors continue to motivate them.

Reinforcement is in the Eye of the Beholder

Reinforcement theory is very straightforward and simple to implement, but it is important to remember that reinforcement is in the eye of the beholder. For example, to get attention, many individuals will act in a negative way to get the attention of a significant other. If they get the attention they are seeking, it ends up reinforcing negative behavior. One company offered lunch with the President as a reward if a representative came up with an idea that increased sales by 10%. However, the President was a tyrant and nobody wanted to have lunch with him, so the reward was actually a punishment rather than reinforcement.

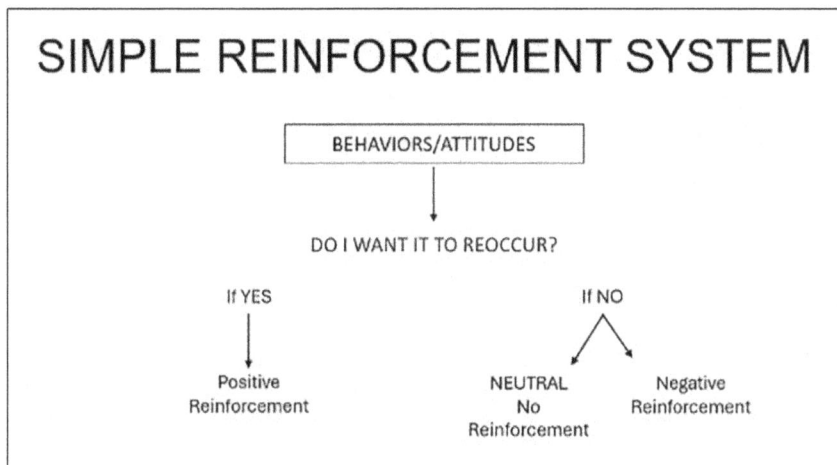

SIMPLE REINFORCEMENT SYSTEM

BEHAVIORS/ATTITUDES

DO I WANT IT TO REOCCUR?

If YES

If NO

Positive
Reinforcement

NEUTRAL
No
Reinforcement

Negative
Reinforcement

When Positive Becomes Negative: A Hockey Lesson

The first example of misaligned reinforcement is from my hockey career. I had a coach who was a disciple of Positive Mental Attitude and believed exclusively in being positive in all situations. After a shift where I thought I played extremely well, he would compliment me, and it was effective as it aligned with my internal feelings of competence and satisfaction. The problem occurred if I had an average shift or performed poorly, as he would give the same positive feedback and compliment me. After a few games, his value as an external reinforcer became irrelevant to me and all the other players who were treated the same way. We were all wondering what game he was watching. He ended up being perceived as reinforcing mediocrity, as the feedback appeared unrelated to performance.

We had another coach who focused exclusively on negatives, and the only feedback we received was for mistakes. We all became consciously incompetent and afraid of making mistakes rather than focusing on leveraging our strengths and playing up to our potential. Both coaching approaches failed because the external reinforcement was not aligned with internal reality or actual performance.

The Alignment Problem

The main problem with developing habits is the necessity for the internal and external reinforcers to be aligned. In performance-based careers like sales and professional sports, it is often confused because of the gap between performance and results and the lack of alignment between internal and external reinforcers.

In sales, this misalignment can occur with the allocation of team bonuses whereby everyone receives an equal bonus regardless of their relative contribution and efforts. The only individuals that benefit proportionately are the average performers. The top performers feel cheated, and the bottom performers continue to perform at their levels. Top performers who feel they are supporting poor performers become disturbable and often seek out alternative opportunities. Losing a top performer is a major loss for any organization.

The Gap Between Performance and Results

The gap between performance and results can be confusing and create problems for both individuals and coaches. For example, a coach who focuses and reinforces only results and overlooks effort might end up reinforcing non effort. A sales representative could have rested a full week with no activity and ended up with two large sales from the effort that was extended the previous week. The coach might ignore the effort and reinforce the sales. The sales rep could also be confused and begin to think that avoiding activity for a week will always result in sales from the activity the previous week. Inconsistent activity will always result in inconsistent sales.

Unintended Reinforcement: The Workshop Example

In running workshops, there was often an individual who would show up late, and some of the participants would laugh and crack a joke about the individual. I would stop the presentation and bring the late participant up to date on the content they had missed. In two-day workshops on the second day, the same individual would show up late with the same responses from me and the participants. It eventually became obvious to me that we were reinforcing his late behavior and it had become a habit. By giving attention and time to the late arrival, I was inadvertently making lateness more attractive than arriving on time.

Birds of a Feather

Another interesting observation on human behavior is the finding that "birds of a feather flock together." Poor performers will always seek out others to support their lack of performance, and top performers will avoid poor performers and seek out other top performers to discuss what is working well and ideas for future growth. In matrix management situations, poor performers will avoid managers who refuse to support their lack of responsibility and continue to search for a manager who will support them, a major waste of management time.

I once watched a struggling rep spend his lunch breaks with the two lowest performers on the team. Within six months, he adopted their attitudes, their excuses, and their performance level. When he finally left the company, nobody was surprised, he had been rehearsing for failure every day at lunch.

Sales Contests: Short-Term Boost or Long-Term Change?

Finally, sales contests are a great demonstration of the difference between reinforcement and motivation. Sales contests will result in short-term performance increases for externally dependent representatives and very little effect on increasing long-term performance. The contest will also increase the short-term performance of internally motivated top performers, and the performance will continue at previous high levels for internally motivated performers after the contest ends. Top performers like to keep score and achieve. The contest simply provides another scoreboard, but it doesn't fundamentally change their internal drive.

The Ideal Motivational Mix: Push and Pull

In summary, motivation activates behavior and reinforcement strengthens behavior. There are two elements to motivation: push or avoidance of negatives, and approach and the pursuit of positives such as goals and success. The ideal motivational paradigm is typically 10% push and 90% pull. Avoidance strategies and fear of failure can motivate some on a short-term basis, but avoidance begins to lose motivational impact the farther we move away from the negative element.

The Lunch Pail and the Money Sack

For example, I knew a manager who would load up a new representative with debt and told them to buy a new car, expensive clothes, and put a down payment on a house so they would look successful. His theory was that the person would work hard to avoid the consequences of not being able to pay his debts. It worked on some representatives, but others failed and left.

I had a hockey coach who used the same strategy. Once, in the final playoff game of a best-of-seven series, at the start of the game we were waiting for him to give us our pep talk. The buzzer went for us to get ready and tie up our skates, but there was no coach. Then the final buzzer went, and just before we got up to go onto the ice, the dressing room door opened and a lunch pail came flying across the floor of the dressing room. Then the coach came in and said, "If you don't win this game, that is what you will be carrying tomorrow." We won.

On the flip side, a good friend of mine was an NHL goaltender playing in a playoff game, and the coach came into the dressing room carrying a sack full of money. He dumped it on the dressing room floor and said, "If you win tonight, that is what you will be carrying tomorrow." Halfway through the first period, my friend, who has a great sense of humor, said to the linesman on an icing call, "Can you throw me that puck so I can see what it feels like?" He hadn't had a shot on goal in the first ten minutes.

So both elements can work on a short-term basis, but the 90-10 mix is best for long-term motivation. Also, approaching success and internal reinforcers are like driving toward the horizon,we never get there. It is a journey, not a destination, and based on dissonance theory, it is motivational as long as the gap between the goal and the performance is 25%.

Building New Habits: The Framework

To bring together the concepts of reinforcement and motivation, we can now demonstrate how to effectively develop a new, positive habitual habit and break an old habitual habit. The Building a New Habit Template outlines the components necessary to build a habit. As highlighted on the next page, we need both internal and external reinforcers before, during, and after the behavior.

BUILDING A NEW HABIT

	BEFORE	DURING	AFTER
INTERNAL	Admission Ticket Commit to 100% of the Controllables		
EXTERNAL			

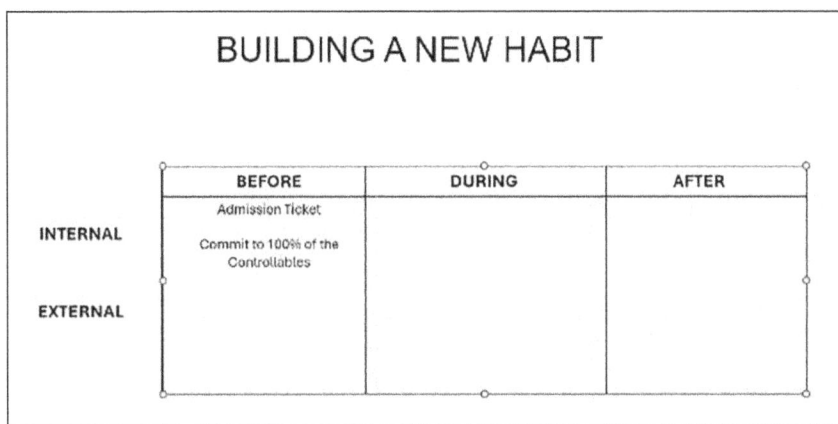

Alignment of Internal and External Reinforcers

In addition, to build a habit, we ideally need to have positive internal reinforcers aligned with positive external reinforcers, and for the reinforcement to occur consistently and as close in time to the behavior as possible.

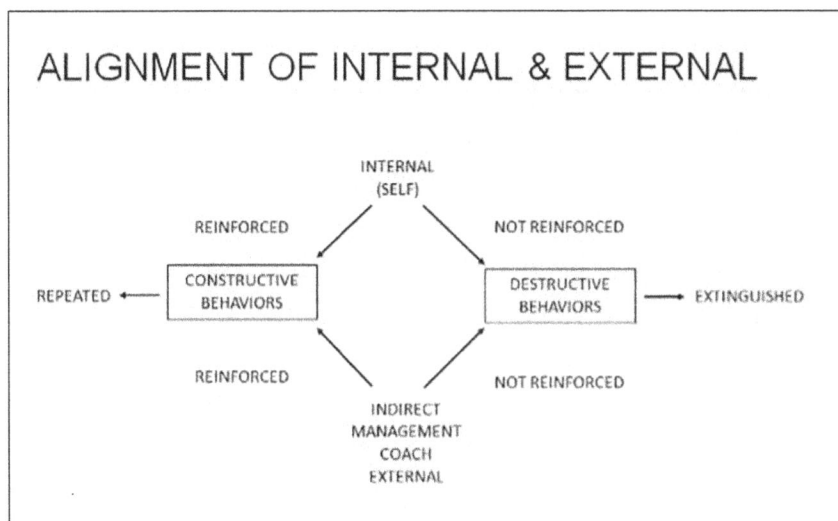

ALIGNMENT OF INTERNAL & EXTERNAL

INTERNAL
(SELF)

REINFORCED   NOT REINFORCED

REPEATED ← CONSTRUCTIVE BEHAVIORS   DESTRUCTIVE BEHAVIORS → EXTINGUISHED

REINFORCED   NOT REINFORCED

INDIRECT
MANAGEMENT
COACH
EXTERNAL

Many individuals make a New Year's resolution to lose weight by going to the gym. I had a good friend who sold gym memberships, and he sold three times the number of memberships that the gym could comfortably accommodate because he knew that only a very small percentage would use the facility on a regular basis.

He knew the gym's secret: most people are great at making commitments but terrible at keeping them. The gym counted on external motivation such as New Year's resolutions, and social pressure. But without internal reinforcement aligned with the behavior, 80% of memberships went unused within three months.

In summary, if all the internal reinforcers and external reinforcers are aligned, as long as we keep our commitment (Admission Ticket) to the 100% controllable activity, we will build a habit because the internal reinforcers will continue to motivate the behavior even if the external reinforcers are not aligned or possibly even negatively aligned. The problem is that internal and external reinforcers can change from positive to negative very quickly. For example, on your way to the gym you get a call from your spouse or manager about a competing commitment. During the workout, your muscles are aching. Also, you notice other members who are in great shape and lifting heavier weights or running faster on the treadmill, and you feel they appear to be judging your workout. After the workout, you get home late and get a cold dinner and a cold shoulder for missing a family commitment. Obviously, many external factors can interfere with developing a simple habit.

Applying Habit Building to Sales Activities

Applying the same process to a sales activity or habit, the same reinforcement principles and alignment can occur. The best example is contacting a referred lead from the sales representative's network. To prepare for the initial fact-finding interview, the representative reviews the information obtained from the referral source and then plans to review the sales presentation with the coach, but the coach is busy and unavailable. An associate drops by and suggests they go out for a quick lunch. After lunch, the sales representative keeps the commitment and sets up the remote presentation and waits for the prospect to connect. The prospect is a little delayed and indicates that they have a drop-dead commitment at the arranged end time. The rep feels a little pressed for time and speeds up the presentation. As we all know, the prospect will pick up quickly on any perceived anxiety. The rep now senses that they are running late and is getting objections from the prospect and is uncertain how best to proceed. To handle the objections effectively requires empathy and time, and the initial interview ends with no commitment to a time for a follow-up interview or meeting. After the call, the coach asks how the call went. The coach might question the content of the presentation or criticize the lack of closing for a follow-up meeting. In summary, the rep kept their commitment and can self-reinforce for keeping the commitment and respecting the prospect's time. However, the anxiety associated with speeding up the call and the objections from the prospect and the negative feedback from the coach could lead to feelings of incompetence and possible call reluctance.

Focusing on Controllables

The only way to avoid developing call reluctance from the negative impact of external feedback from prospects and coaches is to focus on self-evaluating competence based on controllables. The controllables are preparation, keeping the commitment, and execution. The main uncontrollable is the results. As we discussed earlier, the only long-term motivator is a sense of competence. We often hear trainers and coaches expressing the philosophy that every NO is one step closer to a YES. This is obviously not true. To demonstrate, in prospecting, the expectation of a standard sales process is:

10 contacts - 5 initial interviews - 2 closing interviews - 1 sale.

But this can vary dramatically from day to day and could be confusing:

10-8-3-3: In this case, the rep might think they are better than average and don't have to make the 10 contacts to hit the sales target.

10-0-0-0: In this case, the rep could feel incompetent and develop call reluctance.

The only way to prevent call reluctance is to focus on the only controllable (10 contacts), being responsible and making and keeping commitments. In addition to preventing call reluctance, focusing on controllables eliminates the attitude of feeling victimized by external events and losing the internal locus of control we discussed in chapter 2. Often, individuals who feel that they are at the mercy of external factors will stop taking responsibility for the activities they do control. In sales, low locus of control reps will blame poor performance on the economy, the products, the market, the company, the prices, commission structure, etc. This is the reason the gap in performance between low and average Sales DNA and high Sales DNA performers increases during recessions and downturns in the market. The self-directed (high internal locus of control) rep continue to work hard, whereas the low self-directed reps become fatalistic and feel they are victims. Also, low locus of control reps become victimized by any change and not only become stressed but lack resilience and the energy to perform.

The Sophomore Jinx: Where vs. How

The sophomore jinx in sales is often created by focusing on WHERE the results came from versus HOW the results were achieved. Again, the great news about the daily Admission Ticket is that at the end of a year or a quarter, the consistent effort will create a result in terms of the number of sales or revenue. Often when evaluating results, there have been a few lottery sales or whales that have contributed to a major portion of a rep's compensation or bonus. The rep begins to worry about where to find those lottery sales rather than on how the results were achieved. If the rep wants to increase sales for the next year or quarter, they need to either increase the Admission Ticket or work smarter, or both harder and smarter. An interesting finding in psychology is "Action Absorbs Anxiety," and effective action increases performance.

Breaking Bad Habits

Breaking bad habits is a very difficult process as they are being reinforced both externally and internally. To break a habit requires analyzing the current internal and external factors that are maintaining the habit and eliminating them. This appears easy but is very difficult, as the external factors are uncontrollable and will erode any elimination of the internal factors and vice versa. For example, when you decide to quit smoking, you feel worse and often gain weight rather than feeling better. The best method is to replace the bad habit with a competing good habit. Rather than going out after work for a drink, go to the gym. Rather than lunch, go for a walk. Rather than smoke, eat popcorn to replace the oral addiction. Eat fruit for dessert rather than carbs and sugar. Rather than smoke, make your calls to replace the behavior. Listen to a sales training podcast rather than a political one (learn to work smarter).

Creative Reinforcement Systems: Real Examples from Top Performers

Develop new internal and external reinforcers for new and existing habits. For example, I knew a top performer who had an Admission Ticket of 10 contacts a day. Every day he went to the bank and took out ten $10 bills and put them in his left pocket. After each call, he would move one $10 bill to his right pocket and continued until his left pocket was empty. He then deposited the money in an educational fund for his daughter. The physical act of moving money became both a reinforcer for each call and a tangible reminder of his commitment to his daughter's future.

The Number 4 in the Shoe

Another top performer put the number 4 in his shoe. Every day he didn't stop working until he had four referred leads from his network. At the end of the day when he took his shoe off, he would see the number 4. As a successful performer and later as President of a large financial services company, during speeches he would take off his shoe and tell everyone that the number 4 was the secret to his success.

His daughter was dating a sales representative from his company, and one night the rep came to the house to pick up his daughter for a date. He answered the door and asked the rep if he had his four referred leads. The rep said he only had three, so the President indicated that my daughter is not going out with someone who doesn't keep his commitments and told the rep to get another lead or there would be no date. So, the rep went away and got another referred lead and went out on the date with the approval of the President. Needless to say, the President was a successful leader who held everyone to their commitments. The rep is now my insurance agent and financial planner.

Winners Act on Their Authority

The prediction of performance is simply Talent (Potential x Trainable) x Habits (Attitudes x Behaviors).

Notice this is multiplication, not addition. If any factor is zero, performance is zero. You can't compensate for lack of talent with good habits, and you can't overcome bad habits with pure talent. This is why only 17% of salespeople produce 80% of revenue, very few people possess both high talent AND disciplined habits.

Mathematically, if any of the four major factors are low, nonexistent, or negative, it will have a major negative impact on performance. It is difficult to attract, hire, and retain individuals who have all four factors or the potential to develop all four. To be a top performer requires the potential and the habits to maximize and leverage sales potential. Top performers are basically self-managers who are self-reliant, self-motivated, self-reinforcing, self-confident, self-committed, and self-directed. They are totally internal and not dependent on external factors for their performance and success but will accept feedback and coaching from individuals they respect and who they feel can increase their effectiveness.

The foundation of all habit building is this: internal reinforcement will always outlast external reinforcement. You can coach someone, incentivize them, and create the perfect environment, but if they haven't internalized the commitment, the habit will fade the moment external pressure is removed. The Admission Ticket, that daily commitment to controllable activities, is not just a sales technique. It is a philosophy of self-reliance and personal accountability that separates top performers from everyone else. When a sales professional makes their daily prospecting calls not because their manager is watching, not because there's a contest, but because they are committed to themselves and their future, they have crossed the threshold from being managed to being self-managed. That is when performance becomes predictable and sustainable.

Now that we understand how elite performers build the habits that drive consistent performance, we can explore what it takes to keep these high performers engaged and committed over the long term. As we will discover in chapter 7, retention is not primarily about performance, it's about fit. A top performer with excellent habits can still leave an organization if they don't fit with their coach, their team, or the corporate culture. Performance gets you in the door and keeps you employed, but fit determines whether you stayand grow, and become part of something bigger than yourself. The journey from building individual excellence to creating lasting organizational commitment requires understanding an entirely different set of dynamics, which is where we turn our attention next.

" Performance makes you money.
Retention saves you money. **"**

CHAPTER 7

Individual Retention
and Coaching

Predicting performance and retention are very different issues and require different algorithms. As outlined in the previous chapters Performance= Talent x Habits whereas Retention = Fit to the Opportunity which includes fit to the coach, fit to the team and fit to the culture. In our consulting experiences and research, organizations often take a simplistic view of retention which is multidimensional and counter intuitive to reality.

The first factor often overlooked is the difference between retention and effective retention. Effective retention is retaining top performers whereas simple retention includes all levels of performance. As a result, it is easy to fix retention issues if we don't worry about performance. Simply hire loyal, dependable individuals and create a country club environment and retention will be amazing but you might have a performance and productivity problem. However, in a high-performance culture low performers will be terminated or quit in the early stages of a performance-oriented career such as sales. It will now appear that you have a retention problem. In addition, it is important to separate voluntary from involuntary turnover.

Voluntary turnover, especially early in a sales career is typically a Sales DNA fit to the role issue. The low Sales DNA individual quickly realizes that they are not a good fit to the career and possibly to the coach or to the team or to the culture. Involuntary turnover is typically a performance issue. A critical problem in many performance cultures is coaches hanging on to poor performers to make their retention numbers look good to hit their numbers and achieve their bonuses or maximize their compensation plan. We will explore this problem later in this chapter on coaching and team building. Effective retention is often 50% of retention.

The second major aspect of retention that is often calculated to make retention look positive is the difference between retention and rolling retention. Rolling retention is a longitudinal snap-shot whereas retention simply looks at a limited time frame such as annually or quarterly. For example, our strategic plan for our clients in competitive commission-based sales careers in terms of EFFECTIVE 4-year rolling retention is 80, 60, 48, 40. In other words if you hire 100 people, 80 performers will be retained at the end of year 1, 60 at the end of year 2, 48 at the end of year 3 and 40 at the end of year 4. There is typically very little turn-over after 2 years. Before we begin working with a client we ask 2 questions:

1. What is your effective retention?
2. What is your 4 year rolling retention?

Many clients don't calculate either effective retention or rolling retention but do calculate their annual retention rate. An annual retention rate of 60% could be 60, 36. 22, 13% 4-year rolling retention.

Not only is it important to separate retention from effective retention it is essential to track when turnover is occurring. Early turnover is a recruiting or selection issue (i.e., hiring the wrong person) whereas later stage turnover is a fit to the coach or team. With our clients most of the training and survival habits occur in the first 2 years and they have low involuntary turn over after 2 years.

Calculating the cost of turnover is also an interesting exercise and avoided by many organizations. For example, one of my mentors who was the President of a large financial services company once had his actuaries calculate the cost of retaining one top performer based on his 4 year rolling 4 year rate of 17% (before he started working with us) which was the industry average. The cost was $750,000 which included infrastructure costs, recruiting, training, coaching, support, marketing, replacement costs, etc. This was in 1980. Years ago we discontinued our template for calculating the cost of turnover as it was too depressing. It always amazes me that M&A companies seldom include the value of a top performing sales team when evaluating the value of a company but focus only on EBITDA or run rate. The human capital and sales potential of a top performing individual or team is possibly the biggest asset of many organizations.

Involuntary, Short Term Turnover (Performance Issues)

Involuntary turnover is typically a performance issue and a poor fit to the career (i.e., low Sales DNA). In chapter 1 we demonstrated the ROI potential of hiring and retaining High Sales DNA. The second most interesting aspect of the studies was the composition of the existing team. How did so many low performers get on the team and more surprising stay on the team despite the low performance and the negative cost to the company.

This often represents a recruiting problem. As outlined in my previous book 'The Super Sales Recruiter' it could be an attraction issue and the organization is unable to attract a sufficient number of high potential candidates and forced to hire and the coaches forced to keep low performers to fulfil the quota of the business unit. The beginning of the problem is often caused by a failure to clearly identify their Ideal Candidate Profile" (ICP). It is obvious "if you do not know who you are looking for you will probably find someone else." By helping companies identify their ICP we have been able to increase the flow of quality candidates by up to 300%. Al sourcing strategies have also significantly increased the flow of candidates but not necessarily quality candidates which has created a major problem for internal recruiters and hiring managers.

By increasing the flow of candidates hiring managers are forced to filter through increased numbers to find the quality candidates. Unfortunately, quality candidates don't stay on the market as long as average and low potential candidates. As a result, many high potential candidates drop out or receive other offers before recruiters can find and engage them. To hit their numbers, recruiters are forced to hire from a pool of average potential candidates and check a box.

The end result is the Talent Acquisition team hire and retain average and below average Sales DNA candidates to hit their numbers, work their compensation plans and receive their bonuses. Many organizations develop compensation plans that are based on numbers rather than quality numbers. Recruiters and coaches are smart and study their compensation contracts to maximize their income.

In our research, we track the annual number of recruits and the quality of the recruits in terms of performance and retention. It is no surprise that the quality of recruits decreases and the number of recruits increases as we approach the end of a physical or fiscal year. Also, turnover decreases at the end of a compensation year. The numbers are very different when the compensation plans are based on quality recruits.

Predicting Retention from Sales DNA

In our research we also track retention numbers and the cost of turnover. In one recent study with a new enterprise client, they had 42 reps (about 20%) who terminated in the first 12 months. About 62% of the terminations were involuntary. Exploring the reasons for the early terminations demonstrated the problem with hiring average and below average potential candidates. 67.5% were assessed as scoring 3 or lower on our predictor score and stop light prediction model. Green (high potential) candidates which result in the recommendation to proceed with the selection process score 4 or 5 out of 5, Yellow and red (average & low average) candidates whith the recommendation to proceed with caution score 3 or below. 30% had a low EP score which would predict a prospecting problem and 45% had a AP caution which would predict a closing issue. Overall, 75% had cautions concerning performance and retention. If the client had explored these cautions during the recruiting process it might have saved 75% or about 30 terminations. We also track demographic variables to help with both the predictions of performance and retention. The terminators also had less job stability, lower previous income levels, little previous sales experience and were cold sourced. One of the biggest predictors of future retention is the source of the candidate. Warm sourced candidates are typically nominators (existing employees) or centers of influence (individuals who are external to the company but are familiar with the opportunity). It is obvious that warm sources are more familiar with the opportunity and the ICP. The client estimated it would cost about $25,000 to recruit and train the early terminators. This would save $750,000 in replacement costs and replacing the 30 low potential with High Potential sales consultants would result in (30 x $1,063.000) $31,890,000 increase in annual sales.

In summary, low Sales DNA is the biggest predictor of short term, involuntary effective retention. Individuals who are a fit to the role will seldom be performance issues, however, fit to the coach and team will be the major factors in longer term effective retention. One of the major responsibilities of a sales leader is to control who they allow to become and remain part of a sales team. Similar to sales performers sales leaders must be responsible and accountable. If a leader expects others to make and keep commitments they must "walk the talk."

Voluntary Long-Term Retention Fit to the Coach/Leader

Most voluntary terminations are either due to a poor fit between the coach and the representative or a compensation problem. If a top performer is working hard and not feeling they are being compensated for their performance they will seek alternatives especially if there are other poorer performers on the team who are making less but not proportionately less income. Also, if a top performer is not receiving perceived value from their coach or leader they will seek alternatives. Top performers need to be challenged and continue to grow through interactions with their coach. Coaches have a natural coaching style and system that is most effective with individuals who enjoy and excel under a coach who is well matched to their natural coaching and leadership style. We have been able to significantly increase retention and effectiveness by helping coaches understand their natural style and how to adjust their natural coaching style to match the individual needs and Sales DNA differences of their sales team members. This has also helped our clients select the best coach to replace a coach who is retiring or moving within an organization. In the succession planning of sales coaches, to be effective, it is essential to understand the composition of the existing sales team members and the natural style of the coach who is being replaced. To avoid early turnover, the new coach must have a similar coaching style and make up to the incumbent. If the goal of the organization is to maintain the status quo in terms of team performance and make up, the new coach must be selected to replicate the replaced coach. This will ensure a smooth transition and minimum turnover. If the goal is to increase performance or change the current team culture, then the new coach transition will be disruptive and create initial performance and/or retention issues. In our research, if a new coach is brought in to replace an existing coach that has different DNA, all the existing team members will be gone in 5 years. An understanding of the DNA of a sales leader is the first step to explore how a fit to the coach and to the team are the major predictors of long term voluntary retention.

Sales Leader DNA

Similar to Sales DNA, Sales Leader DNA has two major components:

1. Potential DNA which reflects the individual's natural personality traits. While this foundational potential cannot be created through coaching or experience, it can be optimized and developed. Think of it as a person's natural range within which development can occur.
2. Skills, Competencies and Knowledge which can be developed through training, coaching and experience.

Our research indicates that there is typically a low correlation between success as a sales performer and success as a sales leader. A top performer may become a strong manager or may struggle profoundly. That is why sales performance alone is not a reliable predictor of leadership success. Many organizations have learned this the hard way, promoting top performers into leadership roles only to experience the:

"DOUBLE WHAMMY": losing a great salesperson and gaining an ineffective manager.

To avoid this, it's essential to assess leadership potential directly using validated selection assessments specifically designed to predict management and leadership effectiveness.

We've found that sales success often relies on power, while sales leadership requires a combination of power and patience, particularly the patience to develop others. These are different aspects of potential, and not all performers are wired for leadership.

Depending on the role, sales leaders may require unique functional competencies. For instance, in financial services, a leader may need to recruit, train and coach often simultaneously. The traits required to attract and engage high-performing professionals can align with coaching experienced team members. However, the repetitive, step-by-step training of new hires demands a level of patience and consistency that some top performers lack. High achievers can become disengaged from repetitive tasks, they thrive on challenge, speed and action.

The solution? Structure your management team around complementary strengths. Allocate internal or external resources to balance emerging leaders' strengths with others who can cover areas that are not in their natural zone.

There is not only a functional benefit to this but also a chemistry benefit. One of the most powerful predictors of sales success and retention is the fit between the manager and the individual performer.

Certain managers are just naturally more effective with certain individuals. That's why it's important to match on performance traits and then use broader characteristics such as communication style or cultural fit to build a diverse, high-functioning sales team.

In diverse leadership teams, chemistry and cohesion can create performance beyond the sum of individual contributions. We see this in sports all the time: a good player thrives on a new team not just due to skill, but because of the synergy with teammates and coaches. The reverse is also true: a star can falter in the wrong environment. Sales teams are no different. Chemistry matters.

Some top sales performers do have the Sales Leader DNA. The key is identifying them early. Doing so allows organizations to develop future managers strategically, while also ensuring that exceptional salespeople aren't pushed into ill-fitting leadership roles. Instead, they can be offered meaningful growth paths within the sales track, fostering their motivation and continued success. The goal is to elevate the right people into leadership and to keep your best sales talent thriving where they perform best.

Fit to the Coach: DNA Predictor of Retention

As indicated, understanding the natural coaching style and how to adjust the style to match the coaching requirements of an individual performer, requires an understanding of the specific traits of a coach and how to use the Sales DNA as a coaching and training guide.

In chapter 2, we identified the traits that define the makeup and characteristics of the top performers and now we can explore the process to match the coach and performer. We use a neighborhood metaphor to help coaches understand themselves as well as their individual team members. To be consistent with our statistical normal curve we identify 5 neighborhoods and place the coach and the performer into a neighborhood. If the coach and rep live in the same neighborhood the natural coaching and training style will require very little adjustment to be effective. However, if they live in different neighborhoods, the coach will need to adjust their natural style to be effective. This will require energy and the larger the distance between the neighborhoods the greater the necessary adjustment and energy required to move and be effective. This is one of the main reasons coaches burnout. They are using too much energy attempting to adjust their natural style to appeal to individual differences. All coaches have versatility limits. In other words, if the distance is too great it is impossible to have the energy to continually adjust to the differences. If the coach has a team of performers living in or close to their natural neighborhood, they are productive and the team is well coached. We will talk about team building later in this chapter but let's first explore how Sales DNA can be an effective guide for training and coaching.

Building Trusting Relationship

In any relationship whether that be coach to performer or performer to client, to build trust and be trustworthy is typically a 3 stage process: Communality, Competence and Commitment. In the first stage, we typically seek common interests and characteristics to develop the foundation for being trustworthy and trusted. A prospect will not buy from a representative who is not perceived as trustworthy or cannot be trusted. The relationship between a sales performer and coach must start with communality. As a result, if the coach and performer are living in the same neighborhood on the factors that predict performance it will start the trusted relationship, and the coach will not need to adjust their natural coaching style for communality. However, adjusting to the differences will require energy on behalf of the coach to be effective and will require the coach to be self-aware of their own coaching style and the needs of their team members.

The second stage is competence. Both parties must perceive each other as competent. The final stage and the most important for ongoing trust is commitment (i.e., doing what you say you are going to do). The first time a coach fails to deliver on a commitment will be the end of trust. The first time a rep fails to keep a commitment will be the beginning of lack of trust from the coach. In sales, once the commitment is established and not fulfilled such as the survival Admission Ticket habit, the coach can no longer trust any future commitments. If the rep delivers on their commitment, it enhances the coaching relationship, and we will demonstrate the long term impact in the coaching section later in this chapter. For example, expectations for meetings about performance change. The coach can ask "how did your calls go" not "did you make your calls." The coach doesn't worry about whether or not the rep did the activities (i.e., a will problem) and can focus on maximizing performance and results from the activity.

Enterprising Potential (EP) Top performers are competitive, enterprising and goal oriented. For a coach to be effective, they must challenge the top performers by setting goals and expectations that require effort and growth to achieve. The high EP individual also needs to keep growing in terms of the trainable talent component of performance. As a result, the coach must also continue to grow in terms of knowledge, experience and competence. The good news is that coaches learn as much from other top performers as top performers learn from the coach. I have one rep who continually sends me information on the use of AI platforms, new articles and books on sales and sales strategy. It is challenging to learn all the information, but he provides an incredible amount of new information to pass on to other reps. In addition, I am always researching new ideas to introduce to him for both individual and group sales meetings. Being high EP, I enjoy the challenge and growth. It would be very difficult to coach this individual for a coach who lived in a different neighborhood and was in a comfort zone for acquiring and applying new sales techniques and knowledge. As Darwin indicated "if you stop growing you stagnate and die."

Top performers typically reside in the far-left EP neighborhood and are considered proactive and goal oriented and as we move along to the lower end of the normative scale, individuals become more reactive and process oriented. Goal oriented sales reps have the ability to focus their energy toward achieving goals and self-initiating activities. As a result, they have the potential to be good prospectors and business developers. Process oriented individuals on the other hand rely on either the coach or environment to structure the process to create leads. Process oriented sales reps can be effective if the company has a lead generation program that provides a sufficient quantity of leads without the need to complement the number of leads through self-initiated prospecting. Also, point of sale environments such as retail, car dealerships, and commercial real estate presentation offices that rely on traffic for their leads can also be effective, however, in most cases, no companies are totally satisfied with their traffic or lead generation process and the better reps complement their company generated traffic and leads with self-initiated lead generation. A coach must be aware of the potential differences and coach accordingly. To violate our Principles of Reinforcement, we have seen coaches give a higher percentage of leads to poor performers to enhance their performance and basically positively reinforce nonperformers and punish the top performers by reducing the number of company generated leads or traffic allocated to them.

Also, most coaches share this characteristic with top performers and it is the main common characteristic that is the foundation for trust and the prediction of a longer term relationship.

Achievement Potential (AP)

Top performers have a high degree of drive, energy and ambition. They are motivated by money, challenge, people service and recognition and have a high sense of urgency. As mentioned earlier, many coaches share these characteristics but also have the patience to help others achieve which is absent in most top performers. As we move into neighborhoods with less energy and sense of urgency, to be effective, a coach needs to understand the timeframe associated with goal setting and delayed gratification. The greater the AP the greater the sense of urgency and the quicker expectation of results. When the coach and rep are in the same neighborhood they invariably are comfortable with the time expectations. However, a coach who is high on AP coaching a lower AP rep might set an unrealistic time expectation during a goal setting session. They can be on different time planets. The coach might expect the goal or commitment to be accomplished in the next hour whereas the lower AP rep might be thinking next week. It becomes very frustrating for both parties.

The AP also identifies closing style. High AP reps are hard closers and persistently persistent. When they experience objections in the sales process they push through objections as they feel they have uncovered a need and the best way to service the client is to close the sale. This allows them to satisfy the motivational mix of money, challenge and service. They close the sale without sacrificing the relationship. Hard closers are primarily motivated by challenge and secondarily by people and service.

Soft closers score a little lower on the AP scale and are primarily motivated by people and service and secondarily by money and challenge. Thay are persuasively persistent. As a result, they might not push through an objection as they might think that it will interfere with the relationship. They might sacrifice the sale to maintain the relationship. Coaching soft closers is very different from coaching hard closers. Both require a belief in product but the coach needs to help the soft closer understand that when they uncover a need, the best thing they can do is close the sale and reduce the anxiety of a client associated with uncovering the need and not closing. The soft closer often takes longer to hit goals and targets than the hard closer.

The low AP rep is also not a risk taker and would avoid pushing through objections for fear of damaging the relationship and unconcerned with the challenge. They are very difficult to coach as most coaches are either Soft or Hard closers. It is important for a coach to be self-aware and adjust their approach to coaching to appeal to the closing style of the individuals on their sales team. This is another reason it is essential to have both High and Low performers in a benchmark study as PO (People Orientation) and AO (Analytical Orientation) or style factors can be absent or present in both groups. The key to predicting sales performance is identifying the characteristics that differentiate between high and low performers.

Independence Potential (IP)

High IP individuals like to create their own systems and structure and don't naturally look to coaches for feedback or advice. If a coach wants a high IP individual to follow their coaching system they must set expectations early in the relationship. One of my top mentors would always say to high IP individuals" If we work together you need to do it my way to earn the right to do it your way." They would then negotiate commitments and performance standards. The commitments would be the coaches' activity standards to be part of the team and the results would be the sales numbers required to satisfy the investments made by the coach and company. In other words a sufficient ROI. Once both standards were achieved, they would continue to negotiate and evolve both the commitments and results.

Lower IP individuals enjoy and solicit feedback from coaches. A coach must provide the structure and support without developing a dependency relationship with sales rep. To avoid a dependency relationship the coach needs to be asking vs telling as a coaching strategy and gaining commitment vs compliance.

Communication Style: People Oriented (PO) and Analytical Orientation (AO)

One of the major misconceptions about Top sales performers revolves around communication style. I have heard many times people say "you are a really warm friendly person, you should be in sales." Or "you are an extrovert and would be great in sales." Substance, Sales DNA not style predicts sales performance. There are many warm, friendly, people oriented sales individuals who fail because they have nobody to talk to and there are many introverted sales professionals who are very successful.

Communication style is more a coaching and training issue than a major predictor. As indicated earlier, you can be very people oriented and low analytical, or high analytical and low people oriented or high or low on both. The only real problem is if you are extremely low on both. To be successful you require a modicum of at least one. For example, if there are licensing requirements such as Real Estate, you need a little bit of fluid intelligence to pass the licensing exams otherwise most companies have Subject Matter Experts (SME's) to support sales reps in complex product situations.

High AO individuals can earn the trust of clients by being product experts and coaches can develop sales scripts and closing options to leverage this strength and bring in support to further build interpersonal relationships. High PO individuals can focus on building the relationships and coaches can leverage this strength and bring in the SME's when necessary. Sales reps high on both can develop relationships and be product experts. The key to coaching is being self-aware and aware of the strengths and limitations of reps who have the Sales DNA. In our experiences we have witnessed many high potential sales candidates being deselected over style rather than substance.

The second major misperception about predicting top sales performance is the importance of IQ and education. As mentioned previously IQ basically predicts grade point average. AO is more fluid intelligence or the use of IQ and related more to EQ. The only educational factor our research has identified as predictive is the completion of an educational level not the level of education. In other words, if someone started high school or college or graduate work, the predictor is, did they finish or graduate. This reflects making and keeping commitments. As mentioned previously, we had a client in financial services who decided to hire only MBAs and change their sales strategy to seminar selling. The sales leaders felt that intelligent individuals with advanced degrees in business related courses would be great presenters with instant credibility and attractive to a high-net-worth market. It was a disaster that was terminated after 6 months because neither the company nor the MBA could fill the seminars with participants. Again, initiating the front end of the sales process and business development requires the 17% with high Sales DNA.

In summary, Sales DNA can help guide and focus coaches to leverage strengths and maximize potential and performance. To be effective requires self-awareness of their natural style and how to adjust the natural style to develop and grow top performers. It obviously requires less energy when others live in the same neighborhood and are well matched to their natural coaching style. Adjusting style to others requires energy. The greater the required adjustment the greater the necessity for a coach to use energy and versatility to be effective and increase the potential for burnout. Long term retention is highly correlated to a trusting relationship between coach and performer and a function of matching the coaching style to the Sales DNA of top performers.

Coaching for Commitment vs. Compliance

As stated several times throughout this book, top performers are responsible for their performance and accountable for their results. All top coaches develop a system to reinforce responsibility and hold sales reps accountable. It is a relatively simple process to hold individuals accountable but also counter intuitive and often violated. Top coaches spend 90% of their meeting time asking vs telling which is basically the difference between commitment and compliance when establishing goals and performance and activity standards. To demonstrate the process let's look at the first sales meeting with a new representative to establish the admission ticket for creating the initial survival habit of calls.

Commitment Meeting between the Coach and Rep

C "How many calls are you going to do today?"

R «10»

C "Do you have a list of who you are calling?"

R „yes"

C "Are you comfortable with your approach?"

R „yes"

C "Is there anything I can help you with?"

R "No"

C "Great see you tomorrow at the same time"

Follow-up meeting with the commitment kept

C "How did the calls go?" (Note: not "Did you do the calls")

R "Completed all 10"

Summary. The important aspects of this meeting were that the Rep kept the commitment and the coach had the expectation that the rep completed the calls. The coach would now reinforce the rep for keeping the commitment and then explore the content of the calls. For example, "What went well?" Where did you feel most comfortable?" What did you learn through the process?" What would you do differently?" " How can I help?" The meeting would end with "Do you have the list of the 10 you are calling today?" With new reps this would be a daily meeting to establish the AT as a habit and once established as an habitual habit move to weekly meetings.

Non Commitment Meeting between the Coach and Rep

R "I only did 7"

C "You said you were going to do 10? I can't help you if you don't keep your commitments. See you tomorrow to discuss your 10 calls."

Summary. What did the coach learn and what did the rep learn. The coach learned that there is a commitment problem. The rep learned that they will not get coaching time if they do not keep their commitments.

In this situation the coach had to make a decision about the lack of commitment. If the coach had chosen to discuss the calls and reinforce the lack of keeping their commitment, the rep would learn that it is OK and there is no negative consequence to not keeping commitments. The coach must hold the rep responsible and accountable and not reinforce non commitment.

Reinforcing non commitment will result in a chronic problem that sometimes requires tougher sanctions to correct. I learned of two classic examples of an effective coaching strategy to deal with commitment problems from my friend and associate who was the number one MGA with a large North American financial services company.

Despite several short meetings that failed to establish an AT to daily activity with an agent who was barely surviving, at the end of a meeting he handed the agent a letter of resignation and had the agent sign it. He then put it in his desk and told the agent "if you don't keep your commitment you are not going to be successful and there is nothing I can do for you. If you don't keep your commitment, don't bother coming tomorrow and I will sign your letter of resignation." The agent made the decision to keep his admission ticket and became very successful and is still with him. In another situation around Christmas time, the wife of one of his agents called him and said" We don't have any money and we can't afford Christmas dinner or presents for the kids." The manager hung up the phone called the agent into his office, fired him and gave him a check for $15,000. The manager was well connected in the local business community and helped the agent find a more suitable career. The agent is now successful in a different career and remains a good friend.

Compliance Meeting between the Coach and Rep

C "How many calls are you going to do today?"
R «5»
C "To be successful in this business you need to make 10"

This situation actually occurred during a workshop I was presenting with the top producer on the sales team. I asked him what he did. He said he wanted the job so he did 10, 5 for himself and 5 for the coach. So I asked him about the quality of the calls. He said the 5 for me were great and the 5 for the coach were rushed and ineffective.

So the VP of sales was at the back of the room, and he stood up and said. "So John. You are attempting to demonstrate that the real issue is not the size of the commitment but rather does someone keep their commitment." I told him "I wished I had said that." Once a coach establishes that a rep will keep their commitments the goal is to increase the quantity and quality of the commitments. That is basically the role of a good coach, growth and development and hold individuals responsible and accountable. In general, individuals will be much more likely to keep commitments that they have been asked to establish. Compliance is the external commitment that requires coaches to track and enforce and become managers or auditors.

Asking vs. Telling

Many coaches fall into the trap of telling vs asking and believe their job is to solve problems rather than teach others to solve problems. It happens at all levels with many careers in addition to sales. The manager might be busy in the office and a rep will come in and ask "do you a minute to discuss an issue with a sales presentation I am doing tomorrow." The rep will outline the problem and the telling coach will tell the agent what to do. It is a very quick meeting and the coach feels good that a problem was solved and the agent also has the problem solved and has learned that the coach is very competent at solving problems. The rep has also learned that the coach will solve any future problems.

The asking coach will ask "what do you think is the best solution or strategy." What are the possible outcomes:

1. The agent might come up with a better solution than the coach and the coach will learn something.
2. The agent might come up with a good solution that the coach might be able to improve or modify the response by asking additional questions "Would this idea change your approach?" "Have you thought about?"

3. The agent might not have thought about it and the coach might ask the agent to go away and think about a possible solution and come back in an hour.

In this situation the agent has learned that it is important to think about a solution before approaching the coach. The coach has learned that the agent requires additional training or is very skilled at solving problems.

In summary, Sales DNA can help guide and focus coaches to leverage strengths and maximize potential and performance. To be effective requires self-awareness of their natural style and how to adjust the natural style to develop and grow top performers. It obviously requires less energy when others live in the same neighborhood and are well matched to their natural coaching style. Adjusting style to others requires energy. The greater the required adjustment the greater the necessity for a coach to use energy and versatility to be effective and increase the potential for burnout. Long term retention is highly correlated to a trusting relationship between coach and performer and a function of matching the coaching style to the Sales DNA of top performers. The key to retention is developing committed, responsible performers who hold themselves accountable for their results. Top coaches spend 90% of their meeting time asking vs telling, which creates a foundation of commitment rather than compliance. When coaches master this approach, they transform from problem solvers into developers of people who solve their own problems. This is the essence of building individual excellence and the foundation for creating something even more powerful.

Individual excellence, however, is only the beginning of the story. A collection of talented individuals does not automatically become a high-performance team. In the next chapter, we will explore how to build championship sales teams by understanding the difference between Eagles and Traps, and why the lowest performer on your team is actually your real performance standard. We will examine the coaching systems that either reinforce mediocrity or cultivate excellence, introduce the frameworks that separate good teams from dynasties, and demonstrate how corporate culture either accelerates or undermines everything a sales coach attempts to build. Most importantly, we will reveal why retention at the team and organizational level requires an entirely different strategy than retention at the individual level, and how validation data transforms recruiting from an art into a science. The journey from coaching individuals to building elite teams and high-performance cultures is where the real multiplication of results occurs.

> " We need to expect to win before
> we can win. Once we win, we now
> have learned how to win and
> that winning is possible. "

CHAPTER 8

Team Building and Corporate Culture

Similar to top performers, high-performance teams are responsible and accountable to themselves and to their teammates. The role of the coach is to develop a team of high performers through a coaching system that reinforces effort, performance and results. One of the major responsibilities of a coach is who they allow to be part of a team and stay on the team. As evidenced in the benchmark studies, there are several levels of performance on most teams. It is unbelievable that low performers are on the team and are allowed to remain on the team. To explore how this happens, requires an analysis of the makeup of the team and the coaching system. Categorizing the team according to the predictors of performance, Talent x Effort results in the following 2x2 matrix.

In the effort grid we have 4 basic groupings, Golden Eagles who are very talented and work hard. The Effort Eagles are hard workers who require additional coaching, training and experience to maximize their potential. Moving to the right side of the grid we have the Talent Trap group who are talented but don't work hard or have inconsistent effort. The bottom right group are not overly talented, don't work hard and it is miracle that they are on the team.

THE EFFORT GRID

EFFORT

	HIGH	LOW
TALENT HIGH	GOLDEN EAGLES	TALENT TRAPS
TALENT LOW	EFFORT EAGLES	MIRACLE TRAPS

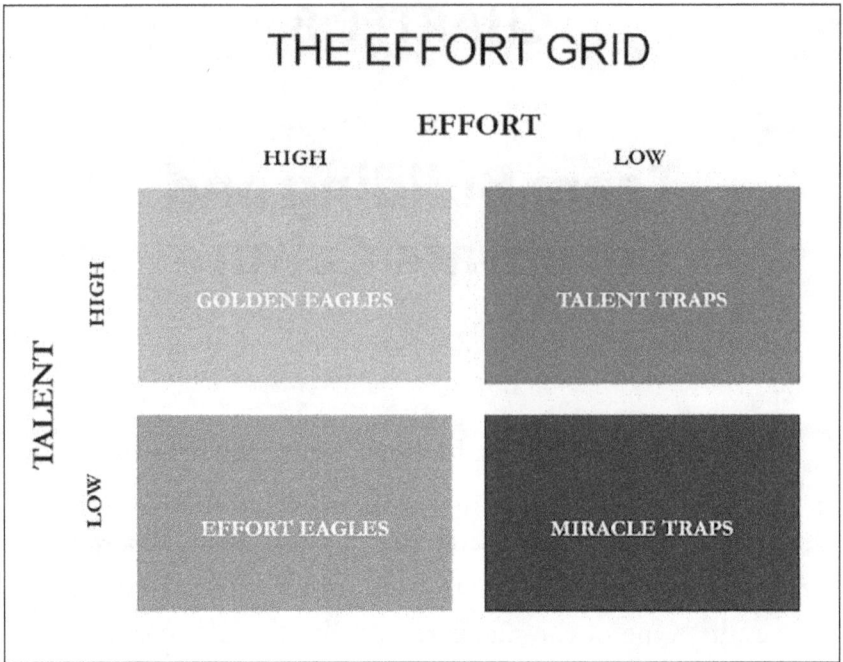

Allowing Traps to be team members is a Selection Problem. A Talent Trap is the result of identifying individuals who are talented and have potential but failed to investigate the habit pattern or work ethic. As we discussed earlier, talent traps have survived and achieved some results through their talent and learned that it is not necessary to consistently work hard to be selected or remain as a team member. It is the coaches' job to maximize their talent but unfortunately they are asking coaches to coax rather than coach. Coaxing is attempting to get a Talent Trap to work hard which is 100% the responsibility and 100% controllable by the individual. Coaches are not trained to be coaxes and by attempting to take responsibility away from the talent traps actually end up reinforcing non effort. As a result, coaches can burnout by attempting to take control over factors they have 0% control over. The Miracle Traps are typically an attraction problem where hiring managers are forced to hire low level candidates because the recruiting system has failed to attract and process potential top performers. In our book AI Super Sales Recruiter we outlined the process to attract, select and hire potential eagles and avoid hiring traps.

The coaching system and coaching standards allow traps to remain on the team and is the main deterrent to creating a high-performance team. When we ask coaches to analyze their current team members and place them into the various categories this starts to identify the performance standards of the coach. As evidenced in the Effort Grid, the coaches AT (i.e., their activity standard} separates the eagles from the traps. However, the fact that the traps are on the team demonstrates that the traps are the real performance standard. The lowest member of the team is the standard otherwise they wouldn't be on the team.

How do we get Traps to become Eagles or understand that they must leave the team if they are not willing to work hard and make the necessary efforts. It is simply by applying the Reinforcement Theory highlighted in our previous chapters. Coaches must develop a system whereby time and resources are focused on the Eagles and to get time and resources they need to start working hard. Top coaches spend 80% of their time coaching Eagles and 20% with Traps. The Traps quickly learn that if they want coaching time they can earn it by working hard which is 100% controllable.

Coaching Golden Eagles is fun as they work hard and get results. Coaching sessions are very positive as the coach can reinforce both effort and results. But they are also challenging as the coach needs to have the knowledge and the competence to help them grow and excel. Effort Eagles are also fun to coach because they are working hard and seeing clients and giving the coach something to coach. In our workshops with top agents, we often find that Golden Eagles like to mentor Effort Eagles as they appreciate the hard work and the desire to grow and improve their performance. They pay the price and earn the right to their time and expertise. They despise Traps as they feel that the Traps are taking up resources without paying the price. The GE are making money and generating revenue that is being wasted on Traps. Because of the waste the company indicates that can't pay the GE any more compensation. This is one of the major reasons that top performers leave a team or company. The second reason is that the Traps lower the performance of the team and damage the reputation of both the team and the company. The reputation and lack of available funds make it difficult to attract other top performers.

The Traps also negatively impact coaching effectiveness and ROI from coaching efforts. The issue with the Talent Traps is they do not work hard or in other words they are a WILL problem. Coaches do not have any control over WILL problems but are well trained and capable of dealing with the CAN problem or with talent development and growth. We have never met an experienced, competent coach who is unable to develop a rep who consistently works hard. Coaches get the greatest ROI from investing in Eagles. Coaching high effort reps always improves results. There is a minimal ROI from investing in Traps as they are simply better trained or more talented lazy reps with no performance increases.

In summary, we find in our workshops that new, inexperienced coaches, often spend more time with their Traps as they feel that the Eagles especially the Golden Eagles are doing well and don't need their time or company resources. They spend 50-80% of their time with Traps which creates 2 problems. The Eagles figure out the coaching system and learn the way to get time and resources is to stop working hard and now the coach has a chronic effort problem. The second problem is the Eagles fly away to other high-performance teams and cultures. It is a common psychological phenomenon" Birds of feather Flock Together." We see this in all performance-based careers, the best want to play on the best teams and for the best companies.

Building High Performance Teams

The coach is responsible for allowing poor performers to remain on the team and develop a coaching system that has performance standards and clearly reinforces performance and results. The ideal coaching system is very simple; allocating and investing 80% of time and resources into Eagles and giving the Traps the opportunity to start working hard and the positive consequences of beginning to work hard and become an Eagle. The ultimate impact on the team will be the reduction in the number of Traps as the Talent Traps will become Golden Eagles and the Miracle Traps will become Effort Eagles. With coaching and experience, effort begins to maximize potential and turns potential into performance and performance into results. The Effort Grid becomes the Results Grid highlighted on the following page.

THE RESULTS GRID

EFFORT

	HIGH	LOW

RESULTS

EXCELLENT — GOLDEN EAGLES

GOOD — EFFORT EAGLES | TALENT TRAPS

POOR — MIRACLE TRAPS

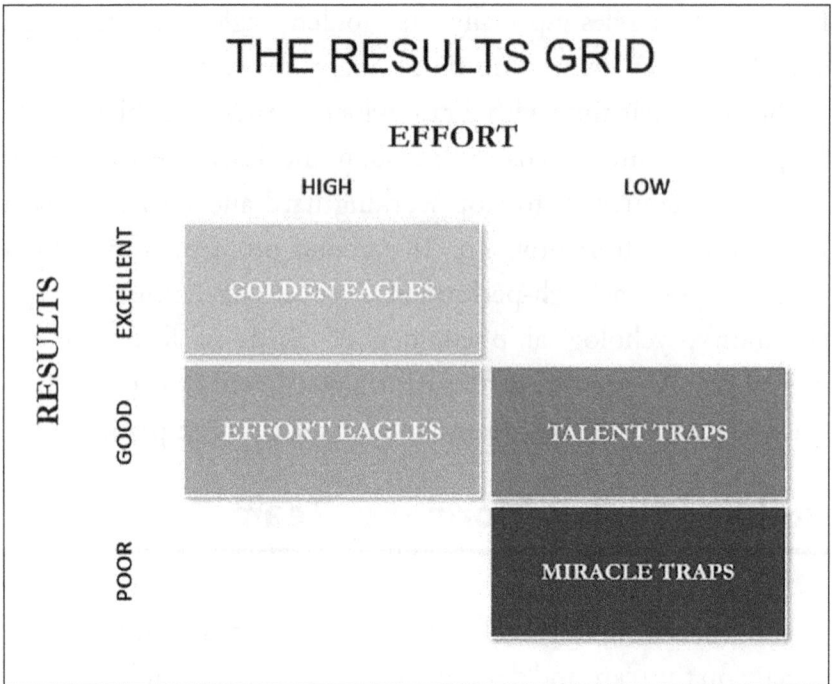

The coaching decision to keep Traps on a team is typically based on ROI. Coaches are constantly assessing the investments they are making relative to the results or return from the investments. The ROI from Golden Eagles is obviously high on both a short-term and long-term basis plus they are fun to coach and as they are creating a number of coaching opportunities through their consistent high levels of activity and client interactions. The coach can reinforce both the activity and the results, and the coaching sessions are positive and require more time. But the time is well spent. The coach also receives compensation for the results and the satisfaction of working with top performers. As mentioned previously, burnout is a poor Return on Energy (ROE) so coaches remain healthy and challenged when coaching

Golden Eagles. The Effort Eagles also provide a good ROI but not as big or as quick as with the Golden Eagles.

When the coach helps an EE with the sales process, the rep will get an immediate increase in performance because the rep is utilizing the skills and knowledge during their high levels of activity and client content. The coach can reinforce the Effort and work on improving the quality of the effort. The Talent Traps tend to create the most stress for coaches. They are getting average results and providing a modest return for the coach because they are talented.

During sales contests, TT often increase their results and the coach realizes they have the potential if only they would work hard. So the trap is that the coach needs to reinforce results without reinforcing the lack of consistent effort. The coach will rationalize the lack of effort by focusing on the results. The biggest negative impact of TT is on the team and Eagles. If the team realizes that the coach only focuses on results or realizes that the way to get coaching time and resources is to stop working hard they might stop working hard to get coaching time especially if they value the time with their coaches.

The solution to the incongruent application of reinforcement theory: the coach must reinforce results but not the effort so the amount of time invested in coaching the TT is far less than the time spent with Eagles. This is a win – win situation for both the team and the coach. The team realizes the coaching system in terms of allocation of resources and the coach can justify the modest returns from the TT by the low amount of time spent on the TT. Also, maybe the TT wakes up and realizes the coaching system and values the coaching time and becomes a GE.

Basically, TT stay on the team providing they are getting results and contributing to the coach's compensation.

Coaching Miracle Traps should be the least challenging for a coach. The ROI from MT is minimal as they are not working hard and getting minimal results. However, the problem and the trap is that most if not all the sales coaches I have met are extremely effective at coaching and can literally make someone successful if they are willing to invest unlimited resources and create a miracle.

As part of our service, sales coaches can call us to discuss the results of our POP assessment on a specific candidate or an existing sales rep. In a recent conversation with a coach that I have known for a long time and have a great relationship, she wanted to discuss a rep who we assessed as having low sales potential but was surviving and getting above average results. She was working hard to prove the prediction of our assessment was wrong and she did. I asked her how much time she was investing and would she do it again. She laughed and said absolutely "no." It is exhausting and not worth the investment of time and energy.

Again, great coaches can make anyone successful, but they might have to wake them up in the morning, get their coffee, help them make the calls, do joint field work to close the sales but they might as well do it themselves. They are also taking away responsibility for performance from the rep and creating a dependency relationship.

In summary, top coaches spend 80% of their time and energy on Eagles and limited resources on Traps. This creates a win-win situation for both the coach and the team. Through a simple coaching system the Traps either make the decision to leave or become Eagles. In addition, on high-performance teams, the team leaders and captains also put pressure on the Traps to become Eagles. The best example is from my experience as a Sports Psychologist with an NHL hockey team. During a team building session, I was presenting the Results Grid and halfway through the session the team captain stopped me and asked the players if they would be comfortable placing themselves and others in the 4 quadrants. Of course, they all said no but realized the only way they were going to win as a team was if all the Traps became Eagles.

I thought it was a great outcome from the session. But the real impact occurred after the session. The team captain called an individual meeting with the most talented player on the team who was a TT and the assistant captains. Apparently, during the meeting they appealed to the player about his importance for the success of the team and they needed him to become the standard for effort and performance for them to become successful. In 2 years, the player went on to become the captain and lead the team to win a Stanley Cup.

If both the coach and players put pressure on the Traps, it is difficult for them to continue to remain part of a high-performance team unless they make the decision to become an Eagle. Again, it could be an attraction problem. The company is unable to attract a sufficient quantity of high quality candidates and instead hire lower quality to hit recruiting targets. It could also be a selection issue that fails to look at the work ethic of a candidate but rather focuses on skills, knowledge and previous experience. Also, in sales, top performers are attracted to other top teams and many companies focus recruiting efforts on attempting to attract top performers from their competitors.

The success of recruiting experienced reps from competitors depends on the fit to the coach, team and culture. It is based on the assumption that "past performance predicts future performance." From our research this is true unless something changes and changing coaches, teams and culture are all major disruptive changes that could have a major impact on the movement of a rep from one team to another. What is true " Past effort predicts future effort." If a person has worked hard in the past they will work hard in the future. Coping with change can be stressful and require additional energy to cope effectively which detracts from the available energy to perform effectively on the job and lowers performance. This can further lead to increasing feelings of conscious incompetence and decreasing conscious competence thereby lowering self-confidence and the vicious cycle of lowering expectations and performance. We will discuss coping with change and maintaining a successful lifestyle later in the next chapter.

Rapid changes in the marketplace can also result in Eagles becoming incompetent. The internet, social media, the pandemic, recessionary periods and AI have all required sales performers to upgrade skills and knowledge. Some top performers have either chosen not to or have been unable to keep up with the growth and development required to perform effectively and adapt successfully to the changes. Again, they haven't changed but failing to keep up with the changes has basically made them incompetent.

Similar to coping with a career change, lifestyle changes can also negatively impact performance. The current Sandwich Generation of having children and at the same time looking after aging parents can seriously impact the performance of former Eagles. The bottom line: sales and any performance based career requires energy.

One final anecdote on keeping Traps. As a hockey coach, I always worried about the effect of cutting players during training camp especially if one of the cuts was a good friend of a top performer. I came to realize that ultimately everyone understands the process to developing the best team and the coach has to make difficult decisions. The key was following a good process and a lot of preparation. I prepared a summary of the players strengths and development opportunities to discuss during the session and encouraged the player to continue to grow and to contact me if he ever needed further discussion.

I would also follow up with a team meeting after all the cuts were made to congratulate all the remaining players and indicate that the cuts were very tough decisions and to book our regular Weekly Development Meeting (WDM) to discuss their individual developmental program and any comments to help build the team. In sales, it is difficult to coach a poor performer who has been referred by one of your top reps or by a high level company executive. This is the reason the process is the most important aspect in dealing with low performers. We are all human and don't like failure or firing someone so the ideal process in team building is to give the poor performer the opportunity to move over or make the decision to leave. From experience if they are not successful it doesn't help them or the team if they remain and continue to struggle. Ideally help them find something they will be good at.

As evidenced, many factors can complicate what appears to be a simple, coaching system to develop a high-performance team. So, one final learning from my experiences is the incredible accomplishment of creating a dynasty or a Championship team or being the best.

Dynasties (Championship Teams)

After another heart breaking loss of our local team to the reigning Champions, the captain of our team indicated that "they lost because they had some passengers." Elite sales teams have no passengers and evolve into a team that looks like the following grid.

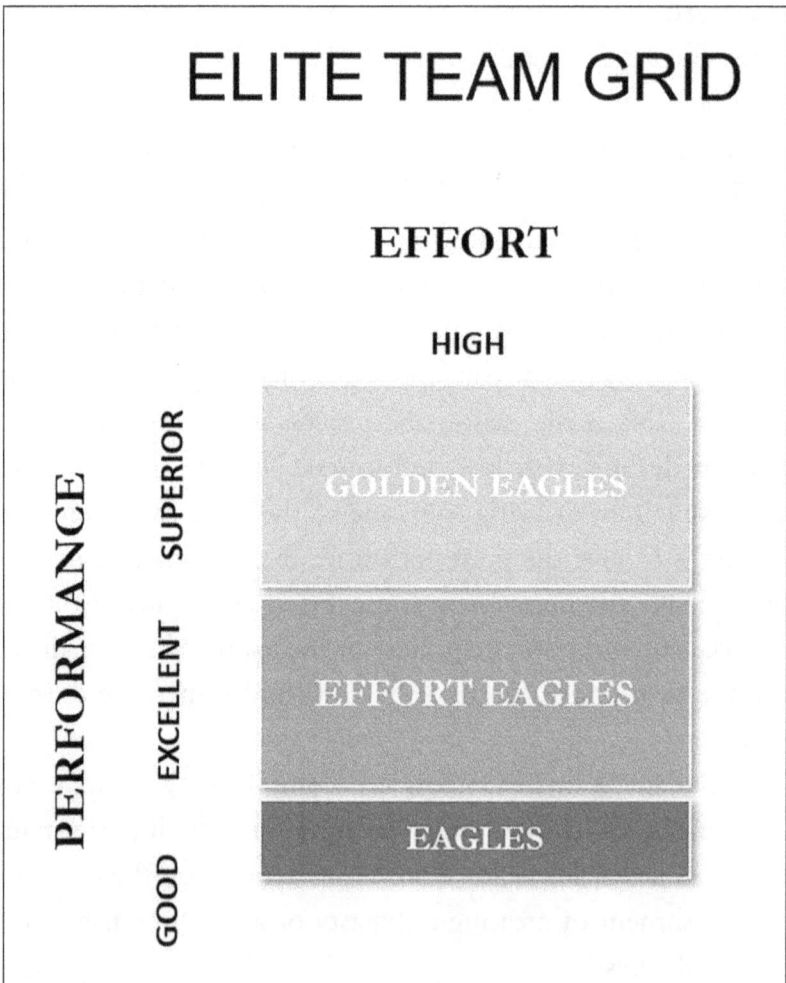

ELITE TEAM GRID

EFFORT

HIGH

PERFORMANCE

GOOD EXCELLENT SUPERIOR

GOLDEN EAGLES

EFFORT EAGLES

EAGLES

A evidenced in the grid for elite teams there are no Traps (i.e., passengers). In any team the lowest performer is the acceptable performance standard. All the team members are performing at a high level and working hard. The Effort Eagles are getting good results through their hard work and as they receive good coaching and experience continue to grow and become Eagles. The Eagles also work hard and grow into Golden Eagles.

In the GE group elite sales teams typically have a few Superior performers that set the effort and performance standards for other team members. They not only provide new sales targets but also break through expectation barriers and set a new standard that is possible to achieve. In addition, the performance of the team and in individual members begins to increase in what is best described as the "Bubble Effect." The team rises upward similar to a bubble rising and setting new performance standards and expectations.

The classic examples come from my athletic experiences and research and include individuals like Wayne Gretzky and Michael Jordan who set new performance standards that were previously considered unattainable. When Wayne Gretzky was traded from Edmonton to Los Angeles, the entire LA team performed at a higher level. In fact, the entire state of California became engaged in hockey. As stated earlier, "If you think you can or you think you can't, you are right."

We need to expect to win before we can win. Once we win, we now have learned how to win and that winning is possible. This directly challenges the counter intuitive theory that you must lose in order to learn how to win. Winning isn't necessarily a habit but it is definitely a goal and an expectation. Success is performing up to potential and controllable, the more successful we are the more likely we are to win. In addition, to establishing new performance expectations, Gretzky set a new standard for effort and hard work. He was the first on the ice for practice and last one to leave. Top performers all work hard in an attempt to master their profession.

The best sales example occurred during a training session with a top financial services organization. One of the products sold by the company was business insurance also known as key person insurance. Basically, it insures the company against the losses that might occur if one of their partners was unable to continue to contribute to the success and growth of the company. It generally provides the income to bridge the gap between the loss of a partner and finding a replacement.

One of the participants was a very successful rep who also helped train new and experienced reps. Part of his role was case discussions and joint field work. During a case discussion, it was established that the rep was going to ask for a million dollar annual premium to cover the key person insurance. This was in the mid 1990s and an annual premium of a million dollars was viewed by the coach as unattainable but agreed to go on the call.

During the client presentation as they approached the close and asking for the premium the coach indicated that he could barely breath thinking about asking for such a high premium. When the rep indicated the premium, the client said, "That is not too bad." He couldn't believe it but from that point forward he had no problem asking for premiums in his own business and helping others establish new standards although very few at the level he had just experienced.

I talked to him after the session and he indicated that top agents started by learning from him and then he started learning from them. The relationship changed from being a mentor to being a consultant. That is the fun and challenging part of coaching Golden Eagles, not only the learning of the coach but also the evolving role of the coach to consultant. All elite teams have at least one outstanding performer that sets new expectations and standards of performance, results and work ethic. As discussed previously. motivation is future oriented. New, higher performance results provide the incentive for future goal setting.

As discussed previously, predicting retention is very different from predicting performance. Early involuntary turnover is typically a performance issue and predicted by a poor fit to the career. The 2 major predictors of longer term retention are fit to the coach and fit to the team. The final predictor of long- term turnover is fit to the corporate culture. The leaders of the corporate culture are responsible and accountable to all the various business units within the corporation, however, the alignment of the revenue generation or sales area with the non revenue generating side of a corporation is crucial for hiring and retaining top performers.

Top performers receive satisfaction from contributing to the financial health of their company but also become frustrated if they feel the money is being wasted on nonproductivity or the lack of support and understanding from the corporate business leaders. It is interesting that very few business CEOs come through the sales or marketing career paths, but all business leaders are aware of the importance of responsible fiscal management and the importance of revenue generation. The remainder of this chapter will focus on the responsibility of the corporate culture for hiring and retaining top sales performers and building a strong sales culture that is aligned with the sales coaches and sales teams.

Long-term Retention Fit to the Corporate Culture

A high-performance sales culture is obviously an essential business unit to developing a high-performance corporate culture. The alignment requires integration with all other business units. To fully explore all aspects of the components would require another book so we will simply focus on the essential components that are directly related to the hiring and retention of top sales performers and the major responsibilities of the corporate culture.

It is often stated that "If recruiting is not your #1 priority it will become your #1 problem." The first step and potentially the #1 responsibility of a corporation is to build a recruiting culture that attracts high potential performers.

"The secret of my success is that we have gone to exceptional lengths to hire the best people in the world!" Steve Jobs

Consistent with the Steve Jobs quote, one of the top priorities of CEO's is retaining and attracting high-caliber people. The positive impact of overall corporate retention and the negative consequences of turnover are major contributors to corporate brand and talent acquisition. Success builds a trusted corporate brand. There is nothing more damaging to a corporate brand than a terminated employee talking negatively to their network about their employment failure and poor treatment whether or not it is justified. On the flip side, everyone loves to hear about and is attracted to success.

We mentioned previously that identifying the Ideal Candidate Profile (ICP) based on performance and retention is essential to building a recruiting culture. This allows a recruiting culture to target potential high performers and build a reputation that attracts other high performers. Building a high-performance culture not only attracts Golden Eagles it also attracts potential clients and customers. Reputation is the foundation of a corporate brand. As one of our clients stated:

"You can't attract Eagles using Buzzards as bait." As part of the process to evaluate a new career opportunity, top performers often request an interview with current top performers to receive more information about the career opportunity.

The 2 characteristics of a Recruiting Culture are:

1. Everyone takes responsibility for recruiting.
2. Capitalize on all available resources.

A consistent finding from our research on attracting top performers is the difference between cold sources and warm sources. Quantity of recruits is from cold sources such as job boards, social media data bases, corporate websites, college placement services and job fairs, whereas quality is from warm sources including nominators and centers of Influence (COI). Nominators are current employees who refer individuals from their networks to career opportunities in their company. Centers of Influence are contacts outside the company who are aware of the career opportunities and refer their networks.

There are many types of COIs, such as small business owners, career coaches, teachers, professors, sport coaches and recruiters from other companies who attract high volumes of quality candidates but can't hire them all. Referencing occurs typically near the end of the recruiting process, and the recruiter simply asks during the process "if you know anyone else who might be interested in the careers at our company, would you refer them to me." It might be no surprise that up to 80% of candidates are cold sources whereas 80% of quality candidates are warmed sourced. The introduction of AI using Algorithms to search and source potential candidates in large social media data bases has further increased the quantity and quality gap between warm and cold sources. Companies are becoming dependent on cold source strategies as they are getting sufficient quantity to check the box on hiring quotas especially if the quality of hires is not being tracked. Many recruiters are now being forced to screen high volumes of candidates rather than lower volumes of quality candidates. Their inboxes are filled with candidates rather than quality candidates. Very efficient but not effective. Warm source recruiting is both efficient and effective.

Setting up an effective warm source networking program requires the application of the principles of reinforcement. The goal of a warm source program is to create a habit of getting referrals from both nominators and COIs and requires reinforcement of the referral behavior. Most of the nominator programs we have encountered offer money to an individual for the referral if the candidate is hired. The problem with this approach is the money is reinforcing the result and not necessarily the activity.

For example, I might refer 10 individuals and only one gets hired so the activity does not get reinforced and disappears. The best programs reward both the activity and the result. There might a smaller incentive for the activity and a progressive strategy for the result. The objection we often get to reinforcing the activity is the potential costs of high volume referral activity. We ask our clients about the sourcing costs to get a candidate into their recruiting pipeline. In one study we performed with a client that was basically receiving 80% of their candidates through cold sources and 20% through warm sources, the sourcing cost was $15 per candidate, $134 per screened candidate and $4100 per hired candidate.

The sourcing costs do vary by the warm and cold source ratios but almost 75% of the hired candidates were warmed sourced. As a result, they could save money by giving a small reward for a referral, such as a $10 gift card for a coffee and still have the budget to reinforce the result of a hired candidate and cover the costs of the increased flow of quality candidates.

My mentor not only reinforced the activity but progressively increased the reward for hired candidates. For the first hire, he hosted dinner at a very expensive restaurant for the individual and one guest, for the second referral that was hired a large gift certificate at a local jewelry store, for the third a clothing allowance at a high-end department store, up to an all-inclusive holiday for 2 at an exotic resort. And, he changed the incentives every year to keep the interest high and the activity high wondering what the next reward might be. He also allowed them to get cash rather than the reward. For COIs he had referral cards with a QR code that he handed out to all potential individuals in his network.

To create the ideal system, he also gave all his employees referral cards to hand out to their networks that allowed him to track and reward both activities and results. He became less dependent on cold sourcing strategies, but the more important point was that the network developed through warm sources was exclusive to him whereas all the cold source strategies were also available to all other companies and recruiters. Also, he discovered that his best referral source was his executive assistant.

Another fun activity was taking his management team on a recruiting blitz day. They would meet in the morning for breakfast with a pack of referral cards and plan the day's activities in terms of the companies, stores, colleges, sports teams they were planning on visiting as well plans for a paid lunch. At the end of the day, they had dinner at a local restaurant to review the day and celebrate together. It became a fun team building session and they received a lot of leads. One of the main reasons this worked well for recruiting sales professionals is that Sales DNA and sales potential can be present in any career path and at any stage of a career and not dependent on any specific academic degree or achievement.

For example, our top sales performer of all time was a CEO of 2 different large financial services corporations prior to joining us. Our current top sales rep has a graduate degree in wine marketing and a black belt in Karate. Another current top performer is an intellectual who speaks several languages and is a Chess Master. My long time business partner in our Self-Management training company started to study and read about sales after he graduated from high school and then started a small business before attending a workshop we were conducting on self-management and approached me about joining us. Our top distributor was raised on a farm and built a highway market to sell produce to finance her education.

We have seen top sales performers who were great waitresses, restaurant owners, mechanics, electricians, teachers, data scientists, actuaries, executive assistants, soccer players, football coaches, lawyers, accountants and the list goes on. Some have undergraduate degrees, some no degree, some MBAs, some advanced degrees in sociology and IT. We have seen very successful women re-entering the work force or beginning work after raising a family. That is the challenging aspect of attracting, identifying and hiring the 17% with high Sales DNA. They can be from any background and located anywhere but they all have sales potential and a strong work effort to help them maximize their potential. You never know when or where you will find the piece gold in the pile of rocks.

The second characteristic of a recruiting culture is the strategy to capitalize on all available resources. This is particularly important for marketing and cold source initiatives. I was consulting for a large company in New York and during the cab ride from the airport to Manhattan I noticed a billboard for the client advertising their new product. During the meeting with the client I asked them why they didn't put a simple, unobtrusive statement at the bottom of the ad "For career information go to www.careers at _____.com or call." They tried it and tracked the number of candidates and it proved a successful strategy. We had a restaurant chain that put the career contact information on their receipts and bills. We had several store operations put career contact information on a poster in the front window of their storefront.

One of our clients set up a career assessment desk with a computer in their reception area so their customers and any visiting vendors/salespeople could apply online. They completed our POP assessment and immediately received our candidate feedback giving them valuable career planning information as a way of saying thank you for taking the time to complete the assessment. The company received a report that evaluated the candidate relative to the ICP profile that predicted the performance potential for their sales culture. The President of one of our clients sold a dealership on donating a car that he put in the lobby of their office building and gave all employees referral cards that they put into a drum and at the end of the year a card was drawn and the winner won the car. It was a great event that created a lot of excitement and resulted in a lot of candidates. To reinforce everyone who submitted names he had a free lunch celebration in the company cafeteria.

AUTHOR'S NOTE: As emphasized in my book, *AI Super Sales Recruiter*, all cold source recruiting will eventually be automated and replaced by AI platforms and applications. AI will automatically source, engage, screen, select and interview all cold sourced candidates and leave the final fit interview with the hiring manager. Warm sourced candidates will be the only proprietary strategy that can help efficiently deliver quality candidates to the hiring manager but through the personal networks of the nominators and COIs.

Start with Eagles – Focus on Quality

Our mission is to help our clients hire more Quality candidates. The goal of a recruiting system and talent acquisition professionals is also to hire and retain Eagles. Eagles are easier to train and fun to coach and the business leaders see the increased profits from an increase in top-line sales and reduced costs of turnover. This also requires the simple application of the Principles of Reinforcement. To accomplish this goal, in-house recruiters and hiring managers must be reinforced for Quality over Quantity and be top sales professionals. In our research, on average, only 15% of potential recruits with high Sales DNA are hired by in-house recruiters and hiring managers. Up to 66% of the hires have average potential and result in a system that will result in mediocre sales performance. There are 5 main reasons for the low hire rates of top potential sales candidates.

1. It could be a problem in attracting Quality candidates
2. Recruiters are overloaded with filtering and screening vast quantities of average and low potential candidates
3. Recruiters and hiring managers lack the skills to sell the opportunity to high potentials.
4. Recruiters are reinforced for Quantity over Quality (i.e., checking a box).
5. Recruiters do not receive feedback on the quality of their decisions to learn and improve the quality of their decisions.

Attracting Quality Candidates. In today's job marketing place and the ability of AI to identify and refer candidates from large social media data bases and job aggregators like Indeed it is seldom a problem of quantity of candidates but often a potential problem of quality candidates. Also, in rural areas and smaller urban areas there can be both a quality and quantity problem. This is the main reason it is essential to develop a warm source networking strategy of nominators and COIs to complement the lack of quantity in small local markets. The warm source marketing strategy is not only the major competitive advantage of smaller companies but it is also not available to larger companies attempting to compete for talent in the more remote geographic areas.

Overloaded Recruiters. With the increased flow of candidates, recruiters and hiring managers are overloaded and required to filter through a large number of candidates to find the best candidates. The time delay creates drop off of potential candidates but more importantly quality candidates have other options and do not stay in the market as long as lower potential candidates. As a result, the recruiter is forced to evaluate and hire from a pool of mainly average potential candidates

Recruiters lack the skills necessary to sell the career opportunity to high potentials. As mentioned previously recruiters need to be excellent trained sales professionals to effectively engage and hire a high potential candidate. High potential candidates are more difficult to sell as they are often consciously competent and know they have options. A good sales presentation always starts with a fact find that attempts to discover what is important to the candidate rather than simply a features sell.

Many recruiters understandably focus on the quantitative and qualitative aspects of the opportunity whereas trained recruiters also start with a fact find and take a career management approach that also includes benefits (what is important to the candidate). The fact find can be 3 questions: "What do you like about your current career?" "What additional things are you looking for in your ideal career?" "How does our career opportunity fit with your ideal opportunity?" The responses to these 3 questions will give the recruiter all the necessary information to present the career opportunity focused on what is important to the individual.

Some of our clients do a bait and switch. For example " we are going to invest a lot of money training you and providing coaching and support resources, why should we hire you?," It is based on the theory that natural sales professionals expect to sell themselves and that people do not value a career that does not require them to pay a price. Top performers don't want an opportunity that anyone can get. The harder they need to work to sell themselves the more they will value the career. Many feel the bait and switch also assesses their current sales training and effectiveness. One of top sales leaders uses our POP results to help close the sale and hire top potentials. This is his closing statement "You are probably wondering why we are willing to invest in you and how we know you have the potential to be a top performer with us. We have hired a top consulting company that created the assessment you completed during our time together and they have developed a profile of our top performers. You have the characteristics that match the profile of our top performers and we are confident that you will have s successful, long-term career with us."

Recruiters are reinforced for Quantity over Quality (i.e., checking a box). One of the biggest problems is reinforcing recruiters for hiring candidates with no accountability for the quality of recruits. As mentioned earlier, it is far easier to hire lower potential candidates and if the recruiters and hiring mangers feel pressure to hit the recruiting numbers established by the business leaders they will take the path of least resistance. This creates the chronic cycle of hiring, training and coaching average and below average potential candidates and creating a modest performance culture. However, the business leaders are expecting and have committed to high performance results. This starts the blame game of trainers blaming coaches, coaches and trainers blaming recruiters and all thinking the business leaders who set the sales targets have lost contact with reality. It is an easy problem to fix if a company is tracking the quality of recruits by collecting future performance and retention data.

However, this requires an integrated validation process that tracks quality at all stages of the talent acquisition process. This leads us to the 5th problem.

Recruiters do not receive feedback on the quality of their decisions to learn and improve the quality of their decisions. It is interesting that there is typically very little sharing data of data throughout the talent acquisition process on the quality of candidates. We have found that potentially valuable information collected at one stage of the acquisition process is blocked at subsequent stages of the process. For example, the source traits on the POP assessment can not only help with the selection decision, but it can also help the recruiter sell the opportunity. The results can help the trainers customize the training content and help the coaches understand the individual and how to maximize the strengths of each new hire. Finally, they can use the Team POP to build an effective team. However, we find that with some clients the information collected through the recruiting process is not shared with the trainers or coaches. Some clients waste money by contracting a second assessment vendor to provide information for team building when they already have better information through the POP.

Maximizing Retention and Growth through Effective Allocation of Training Resources

Skill Based Companies

The biggest waste of corporate training resources is training individuals with low Sales DNA and potential. No matter how much is invested in a candidate with average potential the best result will be average performance. This often happens with skilled based companies. I was consulting with a large enterprise client and was in a meeting on sales productivity with the CEO and the VP human resources. During the meeting, the CEO asked the VP how much they were investing in sales training and what skills and competencies were included in the training sessions. He then asked what was the ROI in terms of performance increases from the training. He also asked can you indicate how investing in each skill is contributing to sales performance. Basically asking for a business case to justify the investment. There was no pre-post training performance data at either an individual or group level. After the meeting we helped collect data on the impact of the training programs on all new hires. The results demonstrated that the ROI varied significantly depending on the quality of the candidate and on the skills and competencies that contributed the most to improving sales performance. Some of the training content had no ROI. The goal was not to eliminate the training but rather to streamline and focus the training on the skills that improved performance and customize the training to appeal to individual needs and potential.

WLL vs. CAN Issues

The second biggest waste of training resources is assuming that all performance problems are CAN issues when in sales most sales performance problems are WILL issues. In other words, most sales reps fail not because they don't know what to do but because they don't apply what they know through sales activity. We covered this in our habit building chapter. All our clients invest and are very skilled at training the sales process and turning effort into results. If a recruit has high Sales DNA, receives sales training and works hard it is almost impossible to fail.

Training all Reps with the Same Program

In our consulting with sales individuals, one of the biggest complaints we get is from experienced successful agents who are forced to go through the same training programs as new or underperforming reps. It is a waste of valuable sales time for high performers and a waste of corporate resources. At a certain stage of an experienced, high performer's career group sales training sessions are a waste of time. Sales meetings introducing new concepts such as changes in compensation plans and new products are always important but group sales training is of limited value as top performers are constantly growing and developing through their own initiative. If they identify a growth opportunity they will seek out coaching and resources to facilitate the growth requirement. Top performers do enjoy sharing their experiences and knowledge with new recruits and existing reps who are working hard and want to grow.

Retention and Compensation – Reward Performance, Don't Punish it

One day, I received a call from one of the players I had coached at university and he wanted to have lunch. He was an average player with great character, a hard worker and fun to coach. During lunch he indicated that after he graduated he joined a top office products and systems company and was the number 2 sales performer in North America. It was a high pressure, competitive, commissioned based career that set high monthly performance standards. He loved the job, had a good relationship with his coach, a tremendous growing client base (lots of referrals) and believed the company products and systems were superior.

However, he was just informed that they were cutting his territory in half and giving half to a new rep. He asked for my advice. We agreed that the most important thing for him to do was to continue to work hard and to hit his sales targets to see if it would work out and after a few months evaluate whether he was still enjoying the career with his current company.

After 3 months he phoned and indicated he was doing well but not as satisfied with the opportunity, so we agreed that it was important to work hard and take a few hours each week to explore alternatives. In 2 weeks he had developed 2 very attractive career opportunities but decided to quit his current job and start his own specialty juice bottling company. After 5 years, he sold his company to a large, international conglomerate and is now quite wealthy.

Writing this book and thinking back on his situation, I wonder who made the counter intuitive decision to cut his territory. I learned that you put your best sales reps in your best territory and never cap the earning potential of a top performer. Also, individuals who have Sales DNA, work hard and can sell, have the most portable skills and job security. Every company and sales leader is looking for top sales performers. This is especially true of commissioned sales reps who realize that their security and earning potential is in their ability to sell and not dependent on a salary or a corporate structure. They are basically in control of their career path. In this case, the company actually punished him for superior performance and lost a top performer.

We had a client who recruited commissioned based sales reps and offered training bonuses in the first 6 months and then shifted to blending out to straight commission after 6 months. Not surprisingly, they were losing the average potential hires in the 6-9 month time frame. Based on the finding that the turnover occurred when the shift was from salary to straight commission, they decided to change their compensation plan to salary with a small bonus for hitting performance standards. We continued to track the quality of candidates after the new compensation plan was implemented and found that the quality of attracted candidates dropped but the quantity of low potential candidates increased dramatically and put additional stress and pressure on the system to filter through the increased quantity. Also, the overall performance of the sales unit dropped dramatically.

By offering a salary they were now attracting individuals who were attracted to the security of a salary. The second biggest characteristic of Sales DNA is high Achievement Potential (AP) which includes a comfort with risk taking. High AP individuals are comfortable with the perceived risk of a commissioned based career and enjoy the challenge and opportunity to make an income with no cap on potential earnings. Companies can't offer unlimited earnings and high variable compensation if they are paying a salary to individuals who are not performing.

Team Performance Bonus

After a golf game, with a relative who was an extremely successful sales rep for an automotive supply company he indicated to me over dinner, that he was moving into a new commissioned based career in commercial real estate. He was making a lot of money and it would take about 2 years to develop a client base that would replace his current income levels but he was upset with his current company and prepared to pay the price and take the chance. His current company had changed the bonus system from individual to a shared team bonus. He was upset that poor performers were getting proportionately more bonus than him. He made the move and is now a very successful in commercial real estate. Again, it is a classic example of reinforcing mediocrity rather than meritocracy.

Coaches Compensation and Retention

One of the major lessons through my years of working with sales coaches and leaders is that they are very smart and know how to maximize their compensation package. For example, if they are being compensated for the size of their sales team they will hit the quantity target at the end of the fiscal period. This is one of the main reasons we see the number of candidates increasing dramatically near the end of their fiscal year and often accompanied by a reduction in the quality of candidates. A focus on quantity with no negative consequence for quality will always create this result.

The simple solution is to change the compensation plan to reward quality and create a negative consequence to poor quality. This simple solution is profitable for both the coach and the company. For example, if the compensation plan rewards a coach for an individual who is performing up to standard at 3 or 6 months, the company will have more money to reward the coach, and the rep will also stay as they are making money. One of our clients implemented a charge back of $10,000 to a coach for a rep who did not perform up to the 3 or 6 month performance standards. The rep was also terminated.

This immediately changed the behavior of the coaches. They focused on quality and both production and retention numbers increased significantly. As the CFO indicated, they now have 'skin in the game' for poor quality hires.

Validation – Data to Strategy

The underlying issue to helping the Corporate culture to align with the sales culture is the lack of validated performance and retention data to provide the knowledge and intelligence to develop the actionable insights to determine the strategy for creating a high-performance culture. The hurdles or roadblocks to performing an effective validation process are typically internal to most organizations.

Predictive validation requires data and measurement of each of the 5 steps of the talent acquisition process at both an input and output level. Attempting to get data on performance and retention is either unavailable or deemed inaccessible because of privacy and confidentiality factors. There is also a fear that validation will identify problems rather provide growth opportunities. The results might also challenge some of the strategic decisions. The goal of validation is to identify what factors are predicting performance and retention and how well they are predicting.

It is important to ask the right normative question of "how well" rather than the ipsative question "is it valid." Asking the ipsative question often results in the difference between data and strategy. We have experienced many organizations that have internal data scientists and data analysts who collect data and provide a very professional analysis of the data. As a statistician we enjoy large sample sizes which often result in statistically significant findings that have little or no practical application. However, by identifying what factors and how effective each factor is in the 5 steps at predicting we can develop a customized predictive algorithm and continue to improve the predictability by simply weighting the factors that predict more heavily in the model without taking any additional actionable steps. The statistical analysis can also help streamline the talent acquisition process and management process by eliminating factors that are either nonpredictive or in some instances interfering with the prediction model and are negatively correlated to performance.

The benefits of streamlining the process improve many factors such as candidate and recruiter experience. Why collect data from candidates at any stage of the process if it is not predictive. Why screen candidates on specific skills, experience and competencies if they are not predictive? Why spend recruiter's and hiring manager's time interviewing candidates and collecting information that is not predictive? Why spend money and time hiring and coaching skills and competencies that are not predictive?

In addition to streamlining the talent acquisition process and significant time savings for candidates and recruiters, validation identifies the best sourcing strategies allowing the company to increase the flow of quality candidates through investing in the sources that are creating the best quality flow. It will also help with creating more targeted job postings and help marketing create materials that appeal to the characteristics of top performers. In addition, the results from the study can help load the content and loadings of the AI algorithms to source and engage top potential candidates. This ensures that the loadings on the AI algorithm are predictive and nondiscriminatory which are the 2 main EEOC regulatory requirements.

Validation will also provide recruiters and hiring managers with information on the effectiveness of their hiring decisions. It will highlight what factors are most predictive and suggestions for collecting and including other factors to improve the effectiveness of their hiring decisions. In addition, we always find that some recruiters are more effective and have identified additional factors that are proving to be predictive. Validation becomes a tool to help recruiters share information and learn from each other.

The benefits to trainers and coaches in hiring more quality candidates are obvious and have been highlighted throughout this book.

As Yogi Berra stated, "It's hard to make predictions, especially about the future."

Over our decades of research and consulting with top organizations, we have been able to help them develop customized algorithms to predict performance and retention. Although there will never be a predictive model that is 100% perfect, through our thousands of predictive validation studies and benchmark studies, we have continually learned about the factors that predict sales performance. Predicting performance and retention results in significant increases in profits by increasing the top line and reducing the cost of turnover by improving retention.

With one of our enterprise financial services clients that had a large competitive, commissioned based sales force, each increase of 1% in their effective 4 year rolling retention doubled their bottom line. This demonstrates the potential impact of compounding production increases with the savings from retaining top performers. As evidenced by the Benchmark studies in chapter 1, the ROI created by an efficient and effective system is possibly the best investment an organization can make to create a high-performance sales culture. The alignment of recruiting culture, coaching systems, team standards, compensation strategies, and corporate values creates a multiplier effect that transforms good sales organizations into dynasties. When everyone from the CEO to the front-line coach understands their role in attracting, developing, and retaining Eagles, the results speak for themselves.

Revenue Generation requires Revenue Generators
Revenue Generators require High Sales DNA

> "
> The sales career is demanding
> and requires energy however the natural
> fit allows the performer to act
> naturally and not waste any extra
> energy to be successful.
> "

CHAPTER 9

Managing Energy – Lifestyle Management

As an analytics company with over 4 decades of experience, we have an experienced research team of data scientists with advanced degrees in statistics and psychology. The biggest challenge with bringing new researchers onto the team is moving them from being strictly data scientists to data interpreters, and moving them from being academic to being practical and applied. This involves answering the 2 most important and commonly asked questions when presenting the results from our studies and helping our clients hire more quality sales professionals.

SO WHAT?

NOW WHAT?

SO WHAT? To answer this question requires moving from data analyses to data interpretation. If we cannot answer this question it is simply being data rich and analytics poor. If the study only presents descriptive data it might be very interesting and present knowledge, information and even intelligence but to be useful it must have practical significance and application. Statisticians and data scientists often present results as being statistically significant and it sounds impressive but many statistically significant findings have little or no applied or practical value. For Talent Acquisition professionals, sales leaders and C

Suite executives, the only value is either a top line increase in revenue or a reduction in cost savings from an increase in retention and a reduction in turn over. If the data doesn't predict any KPI's or desired outcomes it is simply interesting.

NOW WHAT? To move from the SO WHAT? To the NOW WHAT? question requires actionable insights that can be implemented to increase value. This step requires data interpreters who can translate data into strategy. Strategy in the revenue generating area of a company and particularly for sales leaders could involve several options such as new products or services, new markets, new sales targets and objectives, and perhaps the most important underlying issue, do we have the talent and resources to implement the strategy and achieve the objectives. As evidenced in the benchmark studies it might require attracting and hiring more quality candidates that have the Sales DNA to achieve the desired outcomes. In sales it also requires an understanding of any additional skills, knowledge, compensation plans and coaching that is required to leverage the existing potential of the sales team.

All strategic change requires energy to cope effectively and prevent burn out and maximize performance. The Sales DNA in terms of talent and work ethic might be sufficient however the second consideration is the capacity or energy available to leverage the potential. The capacity or energy available is a function of 3 main influences that require energy and can be a negative drain on overall energy levels. Every day we run out of either time or energy. We have discussed the importance of fit to the career and to the opportunity in terms of ROI. Now to address the capacity issue it is necessary to shift to Return on Energy (ROE). The third and final piece to both performance and retention is lifestyle considerations and effective energy management.

The Final Piece for a Lifetime Sales Career

To hire and retain top sales performers who become sales professionals for life requires 3 interactive and essential ingredients to prevent burnout and manage career success. The first 2 are related to potential energy drainers on the job and the third is the management of energy away from the career.

Fit to the Career Acting Naturally and a Good Return on Energy

High Sales DNA reps are a natural fit to the sales career and appear to be almost effortless in fulfilling the daily activity commitments required to survive and excel in a demanding career. The sales career is demanding and requires energy however the natural fit allows the performer to act naturally and not waste any extra energy to be successful. It is a grind for individuals who are not a natural fit as they need to use extra to be successful. In our research, all individuals can be successful on a short term basis in any career path but eventually burn our if they are fighting against their natural tendencies. We define burn out as a poor return on energy. The low sales DNA individual can survive and possibly excel on a short-term basis but the grind can wear them on a long-term basis. The self-manager achieves high sales results which provides a high return on their energy. Their ability to be independent and resilient gives them the ability and confidence to survive and adapt to a constantly changing external environment. As a result, they have the energy to cope with change. They actually thrive on change and view it as an energizing challenge rather than a stress producer. They survive with any coach, on any team and in any organization but excel with a good coach, on a successful team and in a high performance corporate culture.

Fit to the Opportunity Well Matched to the Coach, to the Team, and to the Corporate Culture

We discussed the importance of matching the coach to an individual performer in terms of natural coaching style and living in the same DNA neighborhood. When both the coach and individual live in the same DNA neighborhood neither the coach nor the individual need to use extra energy to understand each other and have a productive stress free relationship, Living in different neighborhoods requires both parties to move into different neighborhoods and the greater the gap the greater the amount of energy required to maintain a positive relationship. There is a point where the gap is too great and challenges the versatility limits of both the coach and the individual. Fit to the team and the coaching system in terms of the performance standards and criteria for remaining a part of the team. Low performers and Traps are viewed as a waste of time and energy and create a negative use of energy to rationalize fit to a poor performing team. To be energy efficient also requires a high performance culture. Again, allocation of time and resources to low performers can be a stress producer for high performers and a waste of energy.

In summary we need healthy, energized individuals, teams and corporations to have the capacity and energy levels to successfully implement change and strategy. The final piece is a balanced, successful lifestyle.

A Balanced Successful Lifestyle

Managing on the job energy is a major key to professional longevity. It is obvious that the better the fit to the job and opportunity the less likely the chances for burn out and the higher the productivity. Energy management and longevity also require managing energy away from the job and integrating a sales career into a successful lifestyle. There are many lifestyle considerations that require energy, however, the major ones are self, career, and family and friends as outlined on the following page in the simple lifestyle plan.

To develop a successful satisfying lifestyle requires a quick review of the difference between commitments and commitment. Commitments are external such as commitments to others such as our family, our friends, our neighbors, our associates at work and to our career, volunteer activities, clubs, churches etc. They all require our energy. Commitment or self-commitment is internal and it is simply keeping commitments to ourselves. Self-commitments are the most important and the most difficult to keep because no one else is available to reinforce us for keeping them. The bottom line, if we don't keep our self-commitments and look after ourselves we will not have the energy to look after our external commitments to others and other things.

In a typical and simplest lifestyle plan for challenging careers, individuals invest about 80% of their daily energy into their job or career, 15% into their family and friends and 5% into looking after themselves. In the traditional model, individuals allow energy to manage them. The highest investment which is their career becomes their #1 priority and takes precedent over the other commitment areas and self-commitments become the last priority. We often learn of an individual missing a family commitment such a kid's concert because of a competing work commitment. This occurs despite the individual claiming that their #1 priority is their family. A recurring story is an individual who planned to go to the gym after work but career and family commitments required all their energy and they missed the work out.

SIMPLE LIFESTYLE PLAN

COMMITMENT AREA	% OF TIME/ENERGY	TRADITIONAL	CONTEMPORARY
Job/Career	80%	1	1
Family/Friends	15%	2	1
Self	5%	3	1

In the contemporary model, the 3 commitment areas are all #1 priorities and it is essential to invest energy every day into the 3 areas. The Admission Ticket concept was initially developed as part of a stress management program where investing in yourself is a daily priority. If an individual does not invest in themselves, they will not have the energy to invest in their careers, family and friends. Keeping self-commitments is the only way to remain healthy and have the energy to look after commitments in a busy lifestyle.

On any given day we run out of time or energy. Some days our career requires almost all our energy and the danger is we fail to keep our other commitments. For example, the day was exhausting and required 95% of our energy, so to keep our daily #1 commitments we must still invest 3% into our family and 2% into a self-commitment. This reduces our feelings of guilt for not keeping all our commitments and potentially overcompensating the next day. For example, spending 95% with the family and

5% on ourselves and none on our career. Then we feel guilty because we forgot our career. So now guilt manages our commitments. The only successful strategy is to keep our #1 commitments every day.

As mentioned previously, we define burn out as a poor Return on Energy (ROE). To maintain a healthy lifestyle and avoid burn out requires a good positive return on our energy investments. The ideal return is internal feelings of satisfaction and totally within our control. We need to learn how to pat ourselves on the back and reinforce ourselves for keeping our commitments especially our self-commitments because there are few external factors that reinforce our self-commitments.

This is often the reason we keep commitments to others over our self-commitments as others will pat us on the back or pay us or thank us for keeping the commitment to them. It is the old story of the plumber fixing his neighbors plumbing while his own pipes are leaking. An interesting observation on human nature is that the closer we get to someone the more we take them for granted. We take ourselves the most for granted and our families for granted over our neighbors and associates and as a result will have more commitment to them and the least amount of commitment to ourselves.

To create a healthy, successful lifestyle requires balancing energy management with ROE. An interesting exercise in the self-evaluation of lifestyle is to rate the satisfaction (ROE) on a scale of 5= excellent to 1=poor. For example, if the career is rated poor (1or2) then it might be necessary to seek an alternate career or career opportunities within the current organization to increase the satisfaction levels. Some might also choose to invest less energy into their career and more energy into other areas with a higher return. Any commitment area that is rated average or poor requires implementing lifestyle changes to prevent burn out. When the return is less than the energy we begin to burn out and the bigger the gap the quicker we burn out. When the return equals the energy, we are fragile and minor changes can negatively or positively impact our attitudes and work ethic. When the return is greater than the energy we are on a roll and energized. When energized we can work hard for long periods of time. When we are in an energy deficit even routine tasks can be overwhelming.

Top sales professionals will naturally look after their careers and pay the price through their daily admission ticket to be successful. They will also naturally look after their family commitments if they have the energy reserves, so the key is to keep their self-commitments, so they have the energy to look after others. Stress is the biggest negative energy drain and effective stress management is essential to personal and professional longevity. Coping with change is a major stressor and requires energy to cope effectively. High Sales DNA individuals have high EP scores and the ability to manage their internal environment and focus their energy into results making them resilient to change and burn out. What are the essential ingredients of a stress management program to keep a top performer healthy and successful.

Lifestyle planning is a multidimensional process that continues to evolve as we mature and progress in our careers and our lives. As we grow, we also add commitment areas that can interfere with our self-commitments. Self-commitment is the starting point for developing new good lifestyle habits and breaking bad habits. Counselling and listening to addicts who have been successful in breaking bad habits such as drugs, medications, alcohol and smoking always indicate that making and keeping a 'commit-ment to myself' was the starting point and totally self-initiated. Any process such as behavior medication that starts externally and tries to move internally is seldom successful long term. Most successful lifestyle changes or habits begin on the inside, becoming habitual through self-reinforcement and then external forces recognize the changes and begin to add to the reinforce-ment and further ingrain the habit. One of the best strategies for breaking a bad habit is to create a competing good habit.

One of the most important concepts for developing a satis-fying lifestyle plan is developing the ability or strategy to compart-mentalize the career from other lifestyle considerations. One of my clients had a "Welcome Home John" sign hanging on the rear wall of the inside back of his garage. When the automatic garage door opener opened, it was a reminder that he had left the office and was now home.

Another client, when arriving home walked to a tree on his front lawn and hung his work on the tree and then picked it back up in the morning. In both cases, it was a strategy to help him separate work from his home life. We label this strategy as having triggers to consciously separate the components of a balance life-style. The trigger concept also works on attitudinal changes. For me, when I am driving to the cottage there is a halfway point where I am leaving the city and approaching the cottage. At that point I stop thinking about the office and start thinking about the cottage and recreational activities and developing fun plans for myself and the family.

The unconscious part was I plugged in my favorite Spotify play list or an interesting podcast or an audio book I wanted to listen to. The trigger concept can be used to remind sales reps about important, essential behaviors such as beginning a sales presentation or asking for referrals. One very successful advisor started every presentation with "Good Morning. Thank you for the opportunity to be with you today. I respect your time and want to confirm the time you have available." That was her trigger to thank the individual and get them involved in the first 5 seconds.

Another very successful advisor after closing a sale would close his notebook and put his pen down which was his trigger to ask for referrals " I am excited to work with you and was wondering if you know anybody else who might benefit from my services." Everyone develops their own system and triggers which is the most important point. What works for someone else doesn't necessarily work for you. The script for any sales track must be developed by each individual otherwise it will appear scripted and forced rather than genuine.

This brings us to "Shoulds" which can be guilt and stress producers. Many well-intentioned coaches and associates will offer advice and tell us what they feel we should do. The suggestions is something that has worked for them and feel it should work for you.

For example, you should start jogging to help lose weight and improve your fitness and for some that works. The jogging relaxes them and helps them think about issues in a relaxed state. For others it becomes a stress producer and as soon as they start jogging they begin thinking about losing weight, how their muscles ache, problems at work and come back from their jog emotionally and physically drained. In stress management programs they often teach progressive relaxation as the way to relax and take a mini vacation. In progressive relaxation, a person or audio takes you through a series of exercises where you tense various muscles and then relax and feel the difference. It works for some but not for others.

For example, the speed of the process was too slow or too fast. Or they started with the legs but the tension was in the neck. Or it didn't achieve the psychosomatic benefit of moving from a relaxed body to a relaxed mind (ie the person needed autogenic relaxation that worked on the mind and then moved to the body). If it didn't work, it actually became a stress producer as the individual started to think they must really be stressed because it didn't work for them. Some quitting smoking seminars start with pictures of damaged lungs and use fear to motivate an individual to stop.

It actually becomes a stress producer with the opposite of the intended effect. Similar to developing good sales habits and breaking bad sales habits, lifestyle management starts with self-commitment and self-coaching. That is the reason good coaches ask rather than tell. Rather than saying this is what you should do good coaches ask, "What have thought about doing?" "What have you tried?" "What has worked well?"

Basically, helping a sales rep become a self-coach and develop systems and behaviors that work for themselves. Good coaches offer suggestions such as "Have you tried?" or "I read that this might be a strategy for you to consider." If a coach tells someone what to do and it takes away from the individual being responsible and accountable.

Moving into lifestyle management and helping friends and family to be self-coaches and being responsible and accountable is essential for developing a satisfying successful lifestyle. Parenting or being a good spouse is often a very challenging aspect of an effective lifestyle and energy management program as we can inadvertently become responsible for the behavior of others and end up enabling them rather than helping them.

As discussed in depth, taking responsibility for uncontrollables is one of the biggest wastes of energy. Parents are justifiably protective of their children and positively motivated to help them be successful and deal with issues. This has led to the snow plough parents and the Helicopter parents, where they solve issues for their kids and tell them what to do rather than helping them deal with issues and become self-managers who can make their own decisions and become accountable.

This is the difference between empathy and sympathy. Sympathy is simply reinforcing others for their behaviors and attitudes and enabling them to continue with their current actions and thoughts. Empathy is demonstrating understanding and helping them to be more competent and to think for themselves. In sales coaching we often discuss the concept of an admission ticket as applied to an open-door policy. Many top coaches leave their door open and are accessible throughout the workday to their team members. However, there is a requirement.

When a rep comes with a problem or would like a discussion of a complex case, the admission ticket is they would have thought about the issue and their possible solutions or they have developed their own presentation to the case. Coaches without the admission ticket tell them the solution or how to present the case whereas the coach with the admission ticket asks "What are your potential solutions?" or "Show me the draft of your presentation." The parent also asks rather than tells. From our consulting experiences, telling often creates a chronic cycle of dependency and many issues keep repeating as any slight variation of a problem requires another discussion rather than the individual having the ability to think and behave with minor variations. Effective parents will also follow up after helping a child develop and implement a solution and ask " How did it go?" "What went well?" What did you learn?" and reinforce taking responsibility and continue to help them grow and solve issues on their own.

For sales reps, coaches and parents worrying about what is happening in the lives of their family members is a major stress producer and waste of energy. When we are uncertain whether our child or spouse is capable of handling a current issue it is very difficult to concentrate on the job. Using emotional energy thinking about what is happening at home or at school can obviously interfere with the energy to keep commitments to the job and self-commitments. When we are worrying about something happening at home or at school we often imagine the worst that could be happening. Also, research has indicated that the majority of things we worry about that might happen in the future never happen. Again a major waste of emotional energy.

An interesting characteristic of high achievers with high energy levels is where to invest any excess energy. Excess energy without a focus can begin to negatively impact our health. Many high achievers have a problem doing nothing or simply relaxing. For example, during a vacation where they now have 80% of their energy available to invest elsewhere they have a hard time re-allocating their energy into simply relaxing without a goal focus (ie poor return on energy). They search for activities to invest their energy and are typically successful in creating a high energy, high activity vacation that ideally involves the family.

As the high achiever continues to grow and become successful they will seek out a more complex lifestyle that could include volunteer work, an avocation, church work, hobbies, etc. to increase their satisfaction levels and invest their excess energy. Many investments can fulfill both a self-commitment and a commitment to others. Coaching the kids team or exercising with the family are simple but effective examples. For a more comprehensive discussion of lifestyle planning the reader is referred to my book "Personal and Professional Longevity Under Stress."

In summary, stress management and lifestyle management are an individual process and require everyone to build their own personal stress management program that includes some key ingredients we call the DELI approach. Discovering sources of stress and energy wasters, Evaluating the Stressors, Learning coping strategies and Implementing strategies that are effective. The focus of this book is to maximize the energy levels of sales professionals to leverage their Sales DNA and create the capacity to perform at the highest levels on a consistent long term basis. So a quick look at a few tips that we have picked up over the years from top performers.

Once they have a balanced, successful lifestyle top performers maintain the balance by implementing the "Add on, take away concept." Before they add on a new commitment they must take away one additional commitment" to maintain the balance. It is the old story delegate a new task to a busy person. Successful sales reps are always asked to mentor new reps or present at sales meetings or sales conferences which require extra effort and time to prepare and deliver and can easily become overloaded and lose the balance. Self-commitment is often the commitment that is dropped to become balanced.

Top performers also balance the activities and energy levels during a day. For example, if cold calling or dealing with service issues are demanding and require a lot energy they will do a few calls and reward themselves with an easier task such as returning a follow up call to a new satisfied client. They also have fun activities that are rewarding. I have a friend who is one of those lucky individuals who remembers jokes and I will often call him after some calls for his joke of the day. Balancing and interspacing tough and easy activities can work for some, although I know some reps who front end load all the demanding activities at the start of the day when they have the most energy. That strategy can exhaust others who find the front-end load eats up all their energy and they have nothing left for the easier activities.

All top performers take mini vacations throughout the day. Can be as simple as taking a walk or putting a picture of their summer home in their office which takes them out of the office psychologically for a brief period of time. Surprising a coworker with a coffee can have appositive effect on both the giver and receiver. A putter and balls to practice putting for a few minutes. The list is endless.

The final piece of Sales DNA is managing energy and investing in themselves every day so they have the energy to look after the other important commitments in their lives. They are ideally suited for 2 fundamental reasons. They make and keep their commitments to both themselves and to others. They have a daily admission ticket of investing a piece of energy into their health and well-being. This is not being selfish as it gives them the energy to look after others. It is also not selfless as they are also looking after themselves. Self-commitment moves the discussion from ROI to ROE. Maximizing ROE through daily investments and effective lifestyle management energizes an individual performer and creates a healthy home and family environment that doesn't eat up available energy from outside influences. Having the energy to focus on daily sales activities will obviously lead to higher performance and higher results (ROI).

> The #1 competency of top performers is they are self-managers who are responsible for their performance and accountable for their results.

CHAPTER 10

Searching for the Gold – The Challenge and the Solution

Sales DNA is the foundation for predicting the performance and retention of top sales professionals and only 17% have it. It is the starting point and has 2 main components Talent x Habits (Can and Will) which exponentially define potential. It is set by our late teens or early twenties and once it is set determines the ROI from all future investments to grow and develop the potential. High Sales DNA individuals will provide a high immediate and long term ROI from all training, coaching and corporate investments. Moderate levels of Sales DNA will result in modest returns no matter how much is invested in the individual. It is also the foundation for professional longevity in a performance-based career for the 17% who possess it.

The financial benefits at a top-line sales level, in terms of revenue, are substantial as evidenced in our benchmark studies presented in chapter 1. The 2 most surprising results from our studies are not only the financial gains possible by replacing low performers with high performers but also the number of low performers that are on the team and are allowed to stay on the team despite low and negative returns.

The solution to fixing this problem appears to be very straight-forward: select, develop and retain more high potential candidates and stop hiring low potential candidates. To accomplish the first step to hiring more high potentials it is necessary to define who you are looking for (i.e., the Ideal Candidate Profile- ICP) and where and how to find them. It is obvious that the ICP must be based on performance and retention. In the current marketplace the algorithms of all AI powered sourcing strategies that search large data bases and evaluate skills, job title and experience are validated on hiring rates rather than performance and retention.

This is also true of job aggregators, ATS and HRIS systems. These systems are automated and extremely efficient at filling recruiter inboxes with candidates who are assessed and screened based on the characteristics of the candidates who are hired vs the ones who are not hired. This simply maintains the existing performance levels and retention rates. Through our partnership with Talent Nest, we have validated and loaded the algorithms with the characteristics that predict both performance and retention.

Through validated algorithms we have been able to increase the flow of quality candidates by 300% by targeting the ICP of top, retained candidates. Talent nest is the only ATS that is based on performance and retention rather than hire rates. Through their data collection and analytics Talent Nest helps our clients identify the best sources that generate the largest quantity of quality candidates. As a result, the recruiter's inbox is filled with quality candidates rather than candidates.

A useful metaphor might be the recruiter is searching for the best candidates from the 17% rather than the 17% from the 83% attracted candidates. Sifting through a pile of gold pieces to find the best rather than through a pile of rocks to find the gold pieces. Extending the panning for gold metaphor, Recruiters are immediately assessing the quality of the gold pieces rather than searching for the gold. This maximizes the efficiency of the recruiter as they are focused on quality candidates and have been able to hire up to 10x more quality candidates as they are not spending time searching for the gold but rather exclusively concerned with selecting and hiring the gold.

The sourcing of candidates for a sales career is very different and much more challenging than for any other career path. Unlike many career paths there is no specific academic steam that leads to a sales career. Top sales potential can reside in any and every career path. High sales potential has been found in every academic stream so it is difficult to target graduates who are entering the workforce for the first time or career changers at any stage of their existing career.

The educational background of top performers ranges from high school grads, to Ph.D.s, to trade school grads, to MBAs, to commercial school grads. The academic stream can range from psychology to finance, to technology to law to accounting to administrative to hospitality. Existing career paths have ranged from university professors, to football coaches, professional athletes, executive assistants, waitresses, plumbers, customer service reps, engineers, CEOs, CFOs, greeters, analysts, programmers, career counsellors, teachers, women and men re-entering the workforce, early retirees, recruiters, existing employees, construction workers, waiters, etc.

In addition, very few individuals early in life think of sales as their ideal first career, unless a family member or friend is a successful sales representative. Family members and friends are the number one source for quality sales candidates especially for the first career choice. Most parents and educators tend to promote other career paths such as doctors, lawyers, accountants and engineers. For an in-depth solution to finding top potential sales reps can be found in my recent book, *AI SuperSales Recruiter: Unleashing AI and the Power of a Validated Predictor of Sales Performance.*

This forces many companies to proselytize experienced representatives from their competitors or from companies in similar markets or to search through active job seekers who either can't find a job or have been terminated or are unhappy in their current career. We label candidates who are unhappy with their current career "Career Disturbed." The ideal candidates are typically happy with their current position but searching for a better career opportunity. We label this group "Career Disturbable."

The ideal motivation for a career change is moving to a better opportunity rather than away from a bad situation. Most active candidates are moving away from an unsuitable situation because of a poor fit or for compensation issues. Further reducing the available pool of quality candidates is that first time sales candidates require a lot more investment in terms of training and require more time to ramp up and get sales results. Many companies are either unable or unwilling to make the necessary investments and attempt to save the front end investments and prefer to invest the saved resources in offering more compensation as the main attraction strategy.

Untrainable Talent

To effectively target where and how to source high potential reps it is necessary to develop your ICP or the characteristics of the 17% who have high Sales DNA. This includes identifying both the Talent and habits of top performers. Overall, The #1 competency of top performers is they are self-managers who are responsible for their performance and accountable for their results. The major untrainable component of talent that is fixed in the late teens or early twenties is personality.

High performers are proactive and self-initiating. They do not wait for external structure or coaches to direct their activities, they self-initiate. As a result, they are good prospectors and business developers and pay the price every day in terms of consistent daily activities to ensure survival and success. They set their own goals, establish the necessary activities to achieve their goals, Commit to the activities, keep their commitments, self-evaluate and seek resources to improve on a daily basis.

As a result, they are self-sufficient and maintenance free but rely on coaches to help with growth and development and clear any administrative or political internal corporate hurdles. They demand corporate resources and coaching time. Through consistent high levels of daily activity, they can self-coach and can tell a coach what is working well and where they need help. This maximizes coaching time as the coach doesn't need to guess how to help the sales rep but rather is directed to growth opportunities by the self-coach.

Through self-coaching the high Sales DNA rep also explores resources and other professionals to help with growth and development. As a result, the coach not only learns from the high performer but also needs to continually upgrade to earn the time by providing value during the coaching sessions. They are also annoyed if the coach or company is investing a lot of time or resources in low effort team members. They set challenging goals for themselves and have the ability to control their internal environment and direct their energy into goals and commitments. Being internally controlled and self-reinforcing and self-motivated makes them resilient to change and adapt to a constantly changing external environment. They view change as challenging rather than stressful.

They are high achievers with high energy levels and have a high sense of urgency. They are motivated by a combination of money and challenge and people service & recognition. They are constantly seeking new challenges but also like to keep score and enjoy being recognized by their peers and coaches and company. They self-evaluate and base their performance on controllable factors that are 100% within their control. They are comfortable with conflict and passionate about their product and company. They believe they are helping people and as a result are effective closers. When they uncover a need the best thing they can do for their prospect is help them by closing the sale. This belief in product makes them trustworthy and trusted.

As excellent closers, they are effective at turning activity into results. By being good prospectors and closers, they set new and higher performance and results expectations for other team members. This breaks through existing standards which raises the expectations and limitations of other top performers

They are self-structuring and independent. They can create their own structure when necessary but will integrate with existing structure that facilitates their development and doesn't restrict innovation and evolution. They are typically team leaders or captains that lead through hard work and positive attitudes. They put pressure on other team members to work hard. They elevate the team by setting high performance standards and being a successful role model.

They have high emotional intelligence and are not only aware of and in control of their own emotional states but aware of the emotional states of their clients and associates. This coupled with empathy and the ability to judge the best sales approach in sales situations helps them close at the right time. They have sufficient intelligence to pass licensing requirements and acquire basic product knowledge but will bring in product experts in complex situations.

They self-educate and are constantly seeking resources to improve and maximize their potential.

In summary, high Sales DNA individuals are talented self-managers who: self-initiate, are self-sufficient, maintenance free, able to self-coach, self-reinforcing, self motivated, resilient to change, high achievers, high energy levels, self-evaluating, comfortable with conflict, trustworthy and trusted, and possess high emotional intelligence. They are challenging to identify but are worth the extra resources to attract and hire.

The COVID pandemic has illustrated the importance of self-management in not only sales careers but all career paths. When the shut down from the pandemic occurred and everyone was forced to work remotely from home productivity levels dropped substantially despite the time savings and the extra energy saved from no longer needing to commute. In theory, the productivity levels should have increased so let's analyze the situation from a self-management perspective.

Most jobs and careers before the shutdown were performed in an office or building structure that had direct systems or structure directing activities and further complemented by on-site monitoring from coaches, managers and supervisors. This was on Friday and then on Monday all the structure and direct coaching disappeared, and everyone was now working from home (WFH) and expected to self-initiate and self-manage.

To effectively WFH requires not only the potential but also self-management training. In all careers, top performers consistently perform the basic activities but also self-initiate and innovate to improve both the efficiency and effectiveness of their daily activities. Most experienced, high performers know the specifics and how to do their job better than the indirect manager. Also, most employees work in structured work environments and when the structure and supervision disappeared it was not natural for them and productivity levels dropped.

Self-managers are also internally motivated and self-reinforcing. When I was working with the scouts on the NHL team, the major question they asked was how we assess the character of a player and whether they are internally motivated. The motivation of top athletes starts on the inside not the outside. They were initially confused so we discussed how they could assess it in their scouting reports.

The simple answer is the situation doesn't dictate the behavior or the intensity of the behavior. In other words, internally motivated athletes behave with the same effort and intensity whether the score is 10-0 or tied. Whether it is the first minute or the end of a game. Whether they are on a power play of killing a penalty. In addition, they have the same intensity in practice as they have in a game. The work ethic of great athletes like Michael Jordan and Wayne Gretzky is legendary. In practice, they put pressure on their team mates to work hard with the same intensity as they would display in a game. They were also the first to arrive and the last to leave practice.

The same is true of top sales representatives. They work with the same intensity during recessions, contests and bull markets whether the coach is present, on vacation or at a conference. They perform the same whether they just closed 2 whales, 1 small account or failed to close a whale. It doesn't change their effort and intensity if the coach is seating in their office or if the coach is in Hawaii. This is also great for the coach, as the coach can go on vacation or on a conference and not worry about the performance of the team and what is happening at the office. Again, the starting point for self-management is Inside to outside NOT outside to inside.

Author's Note: Chris Gee, Ph.D., one of our senior consultants and researchers, wrote a blog "Self-Management Potential is on a significant Generational Decline." In the blog he summarized our 40 years of tracking the personality trends of millions of top performers around the world across 40 countries. He summarized the intergenerational changes "what appears to be problematic, is that the same personality traits that are being underdeveloped within successive generations are actually the same traits that are becoming more important and essential among current and future employees. Consequently, we have created a work culture that the next generation (even the current one) is inherently not well suited to (and it's not their fault)." He went on to define self-management "as a multidimensional disposition that reflects one's ability to take ownership over themselves and their performance and be comfortable in autonomous environments." The most alarming finding was that SM potential had decreased by ¾ of one standard deviation between each generation (Boomers vs

GenX vs Gen Y vs Millennials). Putting that into an IQ context, that would be like the average IQ of the population dropping from 100 to 90. He identified one of the major causes as a dependency on technology and a focus on participation rather than performance and results which is the current and future world of work.

In summary, this dependence on technology has created an environment of immediate and continuous external reinforcement such as social media sites providing immediate social recognition and answers to immediate questions rather than thinking about solutions before searching externally. In addition, self-initiated, unstructured play has been replaced by an addiction to technology. In the past, parents sent us out to play and we had to initiate activities to fill the time before we were required to come back when the streetlights came on. Now, most of the activities are structured and supervised

Talent x Habits

The challenge of identifying and selecting top sales potential is further complicated by the attitudinal and behavioral habits of Sales DNA that also begin early in life and through the many external environmental influences, become part of the Sales DNA by the late teens or early twenties. As a result, when high Sales DNA individuals enter the workforce, they naturally work hard with a positive attitude. They are naturally built to be responsible and accountable.

Attitudinal they are upside thinkers. They are always looking for positives If you ask them about their company, coach, or team. They will start with positives before mentioning any negatives. A positive attitude is habitual. They are fun to be around. It is the old saying "Enthusiasm is contagious and so if the lack of it."

They are self-confident and continually looking for growth and development opportunities. Their self-confidence is based on conscious competence (CC) and conscious incompetence (CI). High DNA individuals are aware of their strengths and have the ability to leverage their strengths when challenged or are faced with adversity. This is often referred to as resilience and grit. In times of slumps or recessions they focus on their strengths to ensure survival.

High Sales DNA are also consciously incompetent and aware of growth opportunities and are constantly upgrading and seeking out resources to grow and realize their potential. Individuals who are CC and CI have the confidence to view their incompetence as growth opportunities. In performance-based careers the higher the self-confidence the higher the performance expectation and ultimately the higher the performance

They also are self-directed and have a strong internal locus of control. They believe that effort gets results and that success is earned rather than random. As a result, they never become victimized when external factors interfere with their results but rather continue to focus on the controllable aspects of performance. This not only shortens slumps but also minimizes the impact of external forces such as recessionary market conditions.

They cope well with stress as they look after themselves by making daily self-commitments to ensure they have the health and energy to keep their commitments to others.

Perhaps the most defining characteristic of the Sales DNA is their strong work ethic. In our research all top performers who become successful work hard. Through self-reinforcement they create habits of effort and make the habit "habitual." They self-reinforce by patting themselves on the back for keeping their self-commitments and commitments.

Adding upside thinkers, self-confidence, self-directed, coping well with stress and strong work ethic to the talent, it should be obvious the reason only 17% have the high Sales DNA to be a top sales performer.

Selecting for Sales DNA

The ideal ICP for sales is simply self-managers who have the talent and the habits that predict sales performance. They must have the personality, positive attitudes and a strong work ethic to be in the 17%. Some might have the personality but lack the work ethic. These are your Talent Traps. They have the potential but lack the work ethic to leverage their potential. Many coaches spend and waste hours and resources attempting to motivate high potentials with a bad work ethic or negative attitudes. Motivation is an internal process totally controlled by the Talent Trap and most coaches not only burn out attempting to take control over something the rep controls they also end up reinforcing a rep for not working hard. At a recent training session talking about finding and selecting self-managers, one of the very successful sales managers, said the following, "We have a choice in developing our team, we can either":

SELECT HARD AND COACH EASY OR
SELECT EASY AND COACH HARD.

This was a perfect summary of the value of making the extra effort to find and hire high Sales DNA candidates. Everything works better and is so much easier when you start with Eagles. The second part of the solution is:

DON'T SELECT AND HIRE TRAPS.

Hiring Talent Traps is one of the hardest aspects to prevent because the TT is usually an experienced sales rep who knows how to sell products and services including themselves. They have the potential and know how to sell it. My biggest mistake was hiring a TT so I have learned from experience. We were looking for a rep to build a block of business for our consulting practice. The candidate had excellent potential based on our POP assessment, extensive experience and training with a famous business product company and was extremely skilled at outlining his sales process and activity levels. We couldn't check references as he was employed and didn't want us to disturb his current situation. His online profile was impeccable. It was quickly a disaster as he turned out be a be a very poor fit for us and our opportunity.

Our opportunity was ideally suited to a self-managing consultant who could function in an open, fluid entrepreneurial environment. The mistake was he had the potential but not with us. He was a product rep in a defined territory that required a hard closer in a tightly managed, monthly performance cycle. We were looking for a consultant in a wide open market that could establish a consulting relationship to sell a concept rather than a product and develop referrals for cross selling through referrals both within the organization and externally.

I have found that product sales reps have difficulty selling concept, but concept reps can move comfortably into product sales. Also there are major differences between a sales rep and a sales consultant. A sales rep is mainly suited for a features presentation but there are exceptions depending on the DNA.

The Art and Science of Selection

The key to avoiding selection mistakes is to include 3 interactive components that are 50% science and 50% Art. The 3 components form a Selection Rater to help make selection decisions.

- Validated, Objective Psychometric Assessment – Sales DNA (100% science)
- Structured Interview of Competencies – Attitudes and work Ethic (50% Science and 50% Art)
- Unstructured Interview – Fit (100% Art)

If a candidate is rated high in all 3 areas, we have found a 90% survival rate, 66% if 2 of the 3 are rated high and <50% if only 1 of the 3 are rated high. If all 3 components do not align it simply indicates that more information is required to find out the reason. For me, the toughest decisions are for candidates that have the potential and the habits but don't fit. One of the questions we ask coaches and hiring managers in our hiring talent workshops is which of the 3 components is most predictive. Whatever the response they all could be accurate. For example, some managers are extremely skilled at conducting a structured interview which can out predict the science and the unstructured interview. Some managers have incredible intuition and can out predict the other

2 components. Overall, science is the best predictor across all interviewers because it is objective and systematic which are the essential conditions for accurate prediction. However, no one component out predicts all 3 together. Three data points that are predictive of performance are always more predictive than 1 or 2. For a complete discussion of creating a predictive Selection Rater the reader is referred to my book 'Selecting Sales Professionals."

Lifestyle factors can also influence selection decisions and lead to hiring a Trap or missing a Golden Eagle. For example. It might not be the right time to hire a candidate due to life-style complications. Changing careers requires energy and the candidate could currently be having difficulty coping with their current situation. A career change might further complicate their decision by creating more stress and the candidate could fail due to a lack of energy rather than potential or fit.

Our Stress Coping scale measures whether the individual is coping well with their current situation or experiencing symp-toms of stress. It is important to discover if the stress is work related or the result of other factors. If it is work related, a career change could alleviate the stress and free up additional energy to facilitate a career transition. If the stress is due to outside factors a recruiter can check back later to investigate if the situation has changed and it is now the time for a potential career change. The compensation package might also create timing issues. If the compensation package is a small base with an over-ride or 100% commission, the candidate might not have the current financial depth to survive in the initial stages of building a 100% variable compensation plan.

The final 'not now' factor might be the composition of the existing sales team. If the team already consists of a few candidates early in their first sales career and are requiring considerable training and coaching resources, the coach might not have any available energy or time to effectively invest in another new candidate. If on the other hand, the current team consists of experienced and trained reps, the coach might be able and willing to invest in another newbie. The bottom line is that all new reps require investment and the selection decision is simply: is the predicted ROI worth the investment.

Coaching vs. Coaxing

On a team made up of Eagles, coaches would be able to focus all their energies on coaching rather than coaxing. Coaching is consulting with sales performers on how to maximize their activities and turn effort into higher performance and higher sales results. All the experienced coaches we have learned from are extremely skilled at helping increase the return on effort and daily sales activities. Coaxing is attempting to get Traps to work hard. As discussed, working hard is 100% controllable by the sales reps so coaches would burn out attempting to take control and responsibility for an uncontrollable. Representatives who do not take responsibility for their effort or fail to keep their activity commitments cannot be trusted. This further creates stress problems and energy wasting for coaches when they are away from the office, at home, on vacation or at conferences or in meetings. Traps who cannot be trusted to work when the coach is away results in worrying by the coach about what is happening at the office. This is the obvious problem of creating dependency on coaching time. When the coach is away the discipline disappears with the Traps whereas the Eagles continue to be active self-managers as they are not dependent on the coach for maintenance.

It Is Easy to Coach. Can They Sell?
Difficult to Coach. Will They Sell?

A sales team with only high Sales DNA members has no passengers. All the individuals are talented self-managers who are goal oriented and enjoy competing to be the top performer on the team. The coach can set high activity and high results standards and focus on growth and development. The lowest performer is an Effort Eagle.

TO TRAIN CAN THEY TO SELL is easy but it is impossible to train WILL THEY SELL with a CAN approach. The biggest waste of training resources is training low Sales DNA reps and expecting high returns. The second biggest waste is assuming that all performance issues are skill issues when all almost performance problems are due to low activity or are commitment issues. The result is an extremely skilled representative and little or no improvement in performance and results.

Elite Sales teams always have a leader who complements the coach and pushes team members to work harder and create a culture of resilience and discipline. I was flying to a conference in Las Vegas and I ended up seating beside a huge guy who was also speaking at the conference. He was an offensive lineman for the New England Patriots who was protecting Tom Brady from the blind side. I had just read Michael Holley's book, Patriot Reign, which was based on having 2 years of unlimited access to the inner sanctums of the world champion Patriots. It was the off-season so I asked him about his off-season activities. He said he had an extensive conditioning program that he completed every day. He did it to maintain his own performance standards but he said he knows that all his teammates are also doing their program every day and he didn't want to be the one who let his team mates down. Great sales teams are the same they trust each other and expect all their team mates to work hard and keep their commitments.

Revenue Is the Fuel to Build and Grow a High-Performance Corporate Culture

The immediate impact of only having high Sales DNA individuals on a team is the significant increase in revenue and profits that provides the financial depth to increase quantitative perks such as salary increases, bonuses, incentives, compensation for all existing employees plus the resources to attract and retain new high performers in all roles.

In addition to the financial and quantitative benefits there are many additional benefits throughout all areas of the corporation in addition to the sales areas. Think of the attraction power and the brand recognition of a high-performance corporate culture that only had Eagles in all departments. Everybody in a community would want to know where all these successful, wealthy, healthy individuals worked.

In a high-performance culture there is less human carnage from failure and the stress of dealing with performance issues. We believe that success builds character not failure. Successful high performing employees are self-confident and productive resulting in a healthy relatively stress-free corporate culture.

Human Resources professionals would see a drop in use of their EAP (Employee Assistance Programs) as there would be less stress from performance issues and turnover. They could focus energy on growth and development rather than performance and stress problems. The training department would see an immediate return on new programs, as the high Sales DNA individuals would immediately apply the new skills, knowledge and expertise through daily activity. Talent Acquisition professionals would be able to focus on a high flow of quality candidates generated through warm source recruiting strategies and be compensated for hiring quality as opposed to filtering through a high flow of candidates, checking a box and relying on cold sourcing strategies.

Predicting Retention

A healthy corporate culture is further enhanced and complemented by a healthy lifestyle. High Sales DNA individuals not only make and keep their commitments to their careers they also keep self-commitments and commitments to their family and friends.

High Sales DNA reps are a natural fit to the sales career and appear to be almost effortless in fulfilling the daily activity commitments required to survive and excel in a demanding career. The sales career is demanding and requires energy however the natural fit allows the performer to act naturally and not waste any extra energy to be successful. It is a grind for individuals who are not a natural fit as they need to use extra energy to be successful. In our research, all individuals can be successful on a short-term basis in any career path but eventually burn out if they are fighting against their natural tendencies.

The self-manager achieves high sales results which provides a high return on their energy. Their ability to be independent and resilient gives them the ability and confidence to survive and adapt to a constantly changing external environment. As a result, they have the energy to cope with change. They thrive on change and view it as an energizing challenge rather than a stress producer. They survive with any coach, on any team and in any organization but excel with a good coach, on a successful team and in a high-performance corporate culture.

Short-term retention is a fit to the career whereas long-term retention is a fit to the coach, to the team and to the corporate culture. Top sales professionals are extremely loyal to a coach who understands they do not require a manager who attempts to control them or allows imposters and low performers to remain part of a team or a coach who invests and wastes valuable time with Talent Traps and Miracle Traps. Self-managers will seldom leave a coach who helps them grow and provides the opportunity to accomplish their self-imposed performance standards. As discussed, the coach is also responsible for building a high-performance team. Therefore a coach who understands self-managers and has a coaching system that focusses on performance and results will never lose a Golden Eagle unless the corporate culture is not aligned with the sales team and culture.

A Lifetime Sales Career

In summary, once high Sales DNA individuals find the best career fit, with a good coach, a successful team and a high-performance culture they will be extremely successful and loyal. The #1 characteristic of high performers is high Sales DNA. The

#1 characteristic of high Sales DNA is self-management. Self-managers are responsible for their performance and accountable for their results. They make and keep self-commitments and commitments to others. They maintain a healthy lifestyle and have the potential to excel for a lifetime in a challenging, performance-based career. They have incredible job security as every organization is looking for high performing, successful sales professionals. Only 17% have the potential but they are worth the extra effort to find, attract, hire and retain. Imagine the return to an organization of acquiring an individual with high Sales DNA for a lifetime sales career.

The Solution (Final Thought)

As I learned early in starting a business, revenue generation is the key to survival, success and growth. The key to revenue generation is to Select, Develop and Retain high Sales DNA professionals. They are a challenge to find as only 17% have it but they are worth the investment and effort.

Again, Revenue Generation requires Revenue Generators.

BOTTOM LINE. Hiring high Sales DNA is like Hiring Revenue which leads to Higher Revenues.

The Complete Self-Management Group System

Sales DNA is part of Self-Management Group's (SMG) comprehensive suite of performance and talent solutions. Additional SMG book titles include:

Principles of Self-Management

Managing Effort: Getting Results

Selecting Sales Professionals

Personal & Professional Longevity Under Stress

AI SuperSales Recruiter

To purchase additional SMG books
visit https://bookstore.selfmgmt.com/

SMG's Training Programs –
Enhance learning with SMG's workshops:
MAXIMIZING INDIVIDUAL PERFORMANCE –
Principles of Self-Management
Sales Self-Management
PERFORMANCE COACHING –
Managing Effort: Getting Results
HIRING TOP TALENT –
Attract, Select & Hire Top Performers

PERSONAL / PROFESSIONAL LONGEVITY UNDER
STRESS – *Survive & Thrive*

TEAM EFFECTIVENESS =
Building High Performing Teams

Predictive Science That Drives Performance

The POP™ Suite of Assessments

SMG's industry-leading tools for identifying, developing,
and retaining top performers in sales, leadership, hospitality,
contact centers, and more.

TalentNest™ ATS

A streamlined Applicant Tracking System integrating POP™
assessments to help organizations attract, evaluate,
and hire the right talent.

Build Talent. Develop Leaders. Predict Performance.

To learn more about our suite of products, please visit
selfmgmt.com or talentnest.com or email info@selfmgmt.com.

www.ingramcontent.com/pod-product-compliance
Lightning Source LLC
Chambersburg PA
CBHW021759190326
41518CB00007B/375